Four Theories of the Press

The links between distinctive political regimes and media systems are undeniable. As Siebert, Peterson and Schramm wrote (1956: 1) 60 years ago: 'the press always takes on the form and coloration of the social and political structures within which it operates'. Nevertheless, today's world and politics are completely different from the bipolar era that inspired the ground breaking *Four Theories of the Press*. What are the main changes and continuities that have driven the study of politics and the media in the last decades? How to approach this interaction in the light of the challenges that democracy is facing or the continuing technological revolution that at times hampers the media?

This provocative book explores the main premises that have guided the study of politics and the media in the last decades. In so doing, it gives the reader key analytical tools to question the sustainability of past categorisations that no longer match up with current developments of both, political regimes and the media. In searching for clarification about current discrepancies between democracies and media's distinctive structures or purposes, *Four Theories of the Press: 60 Years and Counting* puts forward an alternative premise: the political-media complex.

Maira T. Vaca-Baqueiro is an associate professor at the Communications Department of Universidad Iberoamericana, in Mexico City, where she teaches courses on media and democracy, public opinion, political communication, and her real passion, research design and methods. She holds a PhD in Media and Communications from the London School of Economics in the United Kingdom, and a MA in International Relations from Syracuse University in the U.S. and a BA in International Relations from El Colegio de México. As seen in this book, her current research focuses on the relationship between political regimes and media systems beyond traditional paradigms.

'Drawing of a rich supply of literature and original thought, Vaca-Baqueiro explores how to overcome the dichotomy of "liberalism vs authoritarianism," which was so important in *Four Theories of the Press*.'

—**Paolo Mancini**, *Professor of Communication Studies, University of Perugia*

Four Theories of the Press
60 Years and Counting

Maira T. Vaca-Baqueiro

LONDON AND NEW YORK

First published 2018
by Routledge

2 Park Square, Milton Park, Abingdon, Oxfordshire OX14 4RN
52 Vanderbilt Avenue, New York, NY 10017

Routledge is an imprint of the Taylor & Francis Group, an informa business

First issued in paperback 2019

Library of Congress Cataloging-in-Publication Data
A catalog record for this book has been requested

ISBN: 978-1-138-06418-8 (hbk)
ISBN: 978-0-367-88945-6 (pbk)

Typeset in Times New Roman
by Apex CoVantage, LLC

To Mauricio, 20 years and counting.

Contents

Tables, Boxes and Figure

Introduction

How do political regimes influence media systems and vice versa? For decades, the relationship between political regimes (conformed by different elements such as governing elites, political parties, public organizations, regulatory frameworks) and media systems (involving not just media outlets and media ownership, but also programming, content, audience structure and viewership) has intrigued academics from diverse research fields, especially in media studies (see for instance: Blumler and Gurevitch 1977/1995; Swanson 1992, 1997; Swanson and Mancini 1996; Gunther and Mughan 2000a; Park and Curran 2000; Hallin and Mancini 2004a, 2012). The traditional view among media scholars and thus a common point of departure is that different political regimes yield different media systems: while democracies facilitate and enhance free and open media outlets, authoritarian and totalitarian regimes impose strict controls over mass communication. Indeed, these sharp divergences about the media's form and role in different political regimes are rooted in contrasting political philosophies and normative paradigms about government accountability and scrutiny, political liberty, civic participation and public choice (Siebert *et al.* 1956). In short, democracies foster political pluralism and freedom of expression; non-democratic regimes restrict them.

Despite this widespread acknowledgement of the relationship between political regimes and media systems, such straightforward assumptions and normative paradigms are problematic. This book shows the challenges embedded on fitting divergent current political regimes and media systems into ideal types and fixed models developed by the traditional literature on state-media relations. It briefly describes the theoretical abstractions that have guided this area of study for sixty years now. Siebert *et al.*'s ground breaking approach to the different media systems emerging from opposing political regimes (totalitarian or authoritarian rules *vs.* democracies) has inspired a great diversity of works on this interaction. Yet, as some researchers point out, this starting point poses some challenges (see for instance:

Nerone 1995; Mughan and Gunther 2000; Scammell and Semetko 2000b; Christians *et al.* 2009). It not only blurs crucial distinctions within dictatorships or democracies, but also imprints a normative stance inspired by the classical liberal model of democracy: the state and the media *should* be two independent entities. On the one hand, governing elites *should* guarantee the media's freedom, autonomy and diversity. On the other, media *should* play a key role in democracy by keeping the citizens informed about political affairs; by critically scrutinizing the exercise of power by the state or other political actors, and by opening the public debate to a diversity of voices. Nevertheless, the more academic research explores the relation between the state and the media in both authoritarian rules and democracies, the more difficult it is to take these conditions for granted.

The Organisation of the Book

The book develops the notion of political-media complex as an alternative analytical perspective to the one imposed by the traditional view about a schizophrenic media (Mughan and Gunther 2000: 3–4): one that in authoritarianism is manipulated and submissive; another that in democracy restlessly promotes freedom and political choice.

Chapter 1 sets the analytical context for and identifies the literature to which this book speaks directly to. For more than sixty years now, the philosophical rationales, normative parameters and (inevitably) benchmarks crystalised as ideal types of media systems that Fred S. Siebert, Theodore Peterson and Wilburn Schramm introduced in their groundbreaking *Four Theories of the Press* (1956), have steered academic research. The underpinning argument is that different political regimes yield divergent media structures and functioning. In trying to adjust a 1950s vision of a world divided in two geopolitical blocks (the free and the oppressed), academics have modified the 'press theories' originally proposed. The result has been a rich (but at times confusing) variety of media systems and typologies that respond to the flaws and pitfalls on Siebert and his colleagues' appraisal, as well as to the needs of different periods of time.

If for so many decades research on the state-media relation has been grounded on two opposing models—'or four, that is, according to how one counts them', writes Siebert and his colleagues (1956: 2)—why is it today necessary to move this approach forward? Chapter 2 provides the rationale for this book: although politics and the media are radically different from what *Four Theories of the Press* assessed, academic research keeps holding tie to the usual dichotomy between authoritarianism and liberalism. Crucial divergences do emerge when analyzing distinctive political remiges, including among democracies. The challenges embedded on approaching to the state-media relation from ideal types of media 'theories' range thus from distortions about how this interaction actually works on day-to-day bases, to analyses that lose sight of the constant tension between macro-level (structure) and micro-level (agency) factors.

Chapter 3 develops this book's proposal. Building on the notion of 'political-media complex' (Swanson 1992, 1997), this section approaches the state-media relation as a supra institution. That is, this relationship is understood as a complex of interactions between different institutional forces: on the one hand, certain institutions of politics; on the other, the media is approached itself as an institution. Admittedly, neo-institutionalists fiercely debate about why and how institutions matter in the study of political life. But rather than privileging one school over the other, the proposal is to centre the analysis on three common assumptions that at their root unify diverse proponents of neo-institutional theory: (1) that institutions are collections of rules and norms that shape individual behaviour and determine the outcomes of political processes; (2) that institutions are structures of resources and meaning that empower or constrain actors' capabilities of action; and (3) that institutions are markers of history, change and stability.

Media and political communication studies have actually rendered key (but disarticulated) insights about these three aspects of the state-media relation: rules, organisational dynamics and patterns of change. Looking at its norms and regulations, different regulatory frameworks (basically grounded on public service or market-oriented premises) emerge as key determinants of different media systems. When the searchlight is placed on the organisational structures and professional routines, scholarship shows that culture and power are at the core of this interaction overcoming merely technical or naturalistic understandings. For their part, studies that focus on diverse trends of change and continuity suggest that all over the world, political communication and media systems are becoming increasingly similar.

Chapter 4 draws on these findings to put the political-media complex at work. As an alternative point of entry to the study of media systems, these pages cut to the question: how did the process of democratisation change the state-media relation in transitional democracies? The approach contests broad assumptions about this interaction merely mirroring fixed normative prescriptions or misguided individual choices (Swanson 1992, 1997). A quick view of evidence coming from previous research on transitional democracies shows that diversity among authoritarian rules was indeed ampler than what *Four Theories of the Press* diagnosed. Plus, the influence of the authoritarian past over the new democratic regime cannot be assumed exclusively as the deadweight of a torturous past over a promising present.

Some Thoughts on Literature, Evidence and Context

As it can be suspected, a wide range of literatures inform this book. It is evident that Siebert, Peterson and Schramm's *Four Theories of the Press* (1956) is its compass: the compilation provides its central argument (the media mirrors the social and political structures in which it is embedded); the dichotomy of authoritarianism *vs.* libertarianism that is at the core of the 'four theories' overlooks the need to search for alternative conceptual frameworks; rigid media systems denote serious limitations to fit any case study into a single categorisation hence the need to move forward. But other literatures (sometimes related, sometimes detached, seldom brought together) are also at this book's foundations. Institutionalism (rational choice, sociological, organisational, historical), democratisation, journalism, media systems and general political communication studies present key concepts and set the ground for an alternative analytical route. A key challenge in what follows has been thus trying to avoid as much as possible a sense of 'everything goes on' when thinking institutionally about the state-media relation. In the end, write Thelen and Steinmo (1992: 15), neo-institutional studies, might 'explain everything until they explain nothing'. Instead of debating about the constraints or benefits of one institutionalism school over the other, the proposal is to centre the analysis on three institutional factors that at their root give neo-institutionalism a unified theoretical stance: the rules, organisational dynamics and patterns of change. The goal is to generate additional evidence on how, and most intriguing *why*, both media and politicians in new and old democracies are (apparently) predestined to unfulfilling the duties in communicating politics proscribed by the liberal-democratic paradigm. If the time has come to sort out these shortcomings, as this book argues, it is necessary to understand the institutional forces that better explain its current flaws and potential dangers.

1 *Four Theories of the Press* and Its Legacy

It seems that this formidable little book will never die. It shows no signs of even fading away. Why is this? It is certainly no due to lack of criticism for its ethnocentric perspectives, its inconsistent structure, its questionable typology and its problematic assumptions [. . . But] maybe that's the way to do a book. Keep it short. Keep it simple. Keep it descriptive. Keep it neatly organized.

> John C. Merrill, *The Four Theories of the Press four and a half decades later: a retrospective* (2002)

'The press [and by press, in this book, we mean all the media of mass communication] always takes on the form and coloration of the social and political structures within which it operates' argue Siebert, Peterson and Schramm in the opening page to their groundbreaking *Four Theories of the Press* (1956: 1). As obvious and simple this statement may seem nowadays, it remains a guiding hypothesis of comparative research on the relationships between political regimes and media systems. But why is this? How did this 'little book' become so influential in the study of the media and journalism around the world?

The following pages critically assess the main premises introduced by Siebert and his colleagues. Researchers might agree or not with the authors, but the fact is that almost every effort to study the interaction between politics and the media on comparative grounds starts by referring how crucial differences among political regimes (their ideology, regulatory framework or the kind of citizens' participation) shape (mainly constrain) media's goals and functioning. In other words, past and current research on media systems assumes that the particularities of political regimes impose a great influence in media functioning and, more critically, restrain their contributions to civic participation and public debate, just as *Four Theories of the Press* established more than a half century ago.

The Need to Study the Relationship Between Politics and the Media

'When you'd ask Ted Peterson how the book had come to be written', Nerone brings to mind (2002: 134), 'his answer was simple and direct: "by accident"'. Nevertheless, when reading the book, it becomes clearer that it was certainly not 'by accident' that its three authors were interested on the 'the press' as mechanisms of influence and power for political or business interests. Here, an approach to the historical context in which Wilburn Schramm, Fredrick S. Siebert and Theodore Peterson put together their ideas about the media in different political settings is useful to explain the (arguable) success of their book. In fact, a short presentation paragraph to *Four Theories of the Press* reads:

> These essays were prepared in connection with a study of the social responsibilities of mass communication which Dr. Schramm conducted for the Department of Church and Economic Life of the National Council for Churches (NCC). The authors are grateful to the Council for releasing these materials for publication apart from the study.

Indeed, these lines acknowledge the real core of the book: the 'Social Responsibility theory of the press'. Wilburn Schramm had actually been working on a research project on the media's ethics and responsibility funded by the NCC when he ran into Ted Peterson (Nerone 2002: 134). They started talking about their respective research projects, and it was when (apparently) 'by accident' the idea of putting together their corresponding findings gave birth to *Four Theories of the Press*.

Throughout the late 1940s and early 1950s, the NCC sponsored different research projects founded by the Rockefeller Foundation on ethics and responsibility. It was in this context that Peterson's assertion that the rise of mass media made traditional libertarianism obsolete made much sense and was practically unrefuted in the book. From its part, Schramm's study on responsibility in mass communication aimed at introducing an alternative view to some influential liberal and secular standpoints about the potential (but unrestricted) power of the media as big corporations and powerful business groups. Schramm's research was, moreover, deeply influenced by his work during the WWII at different U.S. government departments (Navy, War, Defense and State Departments, for instance), as well as a consultant at some governmental agencies (the U.S. Information Agency, the U.S. Air Force, the Army Operations Research Office, USAID) and diverse international organisations during the postwar period. This standpoint allowed him a sharp criticism of the Soviet system, especially regarding the role of the media in terms of propaganda and controlling social effects.

Fredrick S. Siebert was a prominent member of the journalism faculty at the University of Illinois. He and Schramm had worked together on developing a doctoral program and an Institute of Communication Research, both envisioned as links between the professional needs of journalism as part of a buoyant communications industry and the academic research's demands put forth by the Hutchins Commission—officially known as the U.S. Commission on Freedom of the Press (1947) through which a group of prominent scholars wrote a report dealing 'with the responsibilities of the owners and managers of the press to their consciences and the common good for the formation of public opinion' (U.S. Commission on Freedom of the Press 1947: vi).

Siebert's contribution to *Four Theories of the Press* was crucial (Nerone 2004: 22). He gave the book structure and wrote its two pillars: the chapters on the Authoritarian and the Libertarian theories of the press. Actually, 'since the beginning of mass communication, in the Renaissance', reads the second page of the book (Siebert *et al.* 1956: 2):

> there have been only two or four basic theories of the press—two or four, that is, according to how one counts them. We have written four essays about them, but have tried to make clear that the latter two 'theories' are merely developments and modifications of the first two. *The Soviet Communist* theory is only a development of the much older *Authoritarian* theory, and what we have called the *Social Responsibility* theory is only a modification of the *Libertarian* theory.
>
> (original emphasis)

This particular approach to different models of press-government relationships was grounded on Siebert's previous academic research, especially on his *Freedom of the Press in England* (1952). In this work, he presents an analysis of British history to explain changes on the relationship between mass communication outlets (mainly the press) and the governing elites under different political and social conditions. His historical analysis identifies three different periods (although the author called them 'theories'): the Tudor-Stuart, the Blackstone-Mansfield and the Camden-Ersike-Jefferson theory. One year later (1953), he related these periods with three additional 'theories' to describe the modern functioning and purpose of the media, this time looking mainly at the U.S.: the Supreme Court freedom theory, the Hutchins Commission (or the Social Responsibility) theory and the Soviet Communist theory. The main argument behind this reasoning was that different regulations and social settings shape in very different ways the media's contribution and influence into society. Building on this reasoning, Siebert changed his six-theory schema to the four theories that became the outline for the 1956 collective volume. However, in *Four Theories of the Press*, Siebert's original historical and descriptive purpose seems to lose weight by turning into a prescribing list of normative tasks that rule media's contributions to society.

Ted Peterson joined the University of Illinois from Kansas State in the early 1950s. As doctoral student first, and then as faculty and dean of the College of Communications, he worked closely with Siebert and Schramm in developing a better understanding of the relation between the communication system and the society in which it operates (Siebert *et al.* 1956: 1). Peterson's work actually sought to explain these relationships through the analysis of the links between communication, education, readership, participation and media's responsibility [see for instance: *Magazines in the Twentieth Century* (1956), or; his contribution to *The Mass Media and Modern Society* (Rivers *et al.* 1971)]. He wrote the Social Responsibility theory chapter, as said, the real core of *Four Theories of the Press*. Based on the work of and on the responses to the Hutchins Commission about the nature and problems of a free press, Peterson stressed the need to expand on notions such as 'the public's right to know' or 'the public responsibility of the press' since 'nothing in Libertarian theory established the public's right to information or required the publisher to assume moral responsibilities' (Peterson 1956: 73). Quoting the Wall Street Journal's publisher, William Peter Hamilton, Peterson brings to mind that: 'a newspaper is a private enterprise owing nothing whatever to the public, which grants it no franchise. It is therefore affected with no public interest. It is emphatically the property of the owner, who is selling a manufactured product at his own risk' (*ibid*).

As a response to this (quite influential) line of reasoning of the time (1940s and early 1950s), broadly speaking, the Hutchins Commission found three principal factors that alter and thus force a reconsideration of the notion of freedom of the press: (1) a decrease in the proportion of the people who can express their opinion and ideas through the press; (2) an inadequate service by big media conglomerates to the needs of the society, and; (3) damaging practices from the few (business people or politicians) who are able to use the machinery of the press to satisfy their own interests in detriment of the public good (U.S. Commission on Freedom of the Press 1947: 1).

As a consequence, stressed the Commission, there were five things that (apparently any) society requires from its media: (1) to be accurate: 'identify [the truth about] fact as fact, opinion as opinion' (Peterson 1956: 87); (2) to serve as a forum for the exchange of comment and criticism; (3) to present a representative picture of its constituent groups; (4) to be responsible for the presentation and clarification of the goals and values of its society, and last but certainly not least; (5) to provide full access to the day's intelligence (*ibid*: 87–92). With the passing decades, the specific Hutchins Commission's recommendations blurred together and were raised as 'the happy ideal of the eighteenth and nineteenth centuries in a twentieth-century milieu' (*ibid*: 103). That is, 'a belief system that defines the appropriate practices and values of news professionals, news media and news systems [. . .] an hegemonic model of journalism' tailored to a late-nineteenth and early twentieth-century Western vision of mass media (Nerone 2012: 447). Exporting this normative model of journalism along with many others beliefs and practices that the West exported to the rest of the world, developed on what Mancini (2008 quoted by Nerone 2012: 452) refers to as 'stupid normativity': a constrained notion of normative approaches to mass communication steered by an inappropriate application of Western standards to practically any social and media systems.

All in all, the last paragraph of Peterson's (Peterson 1956: 103) contribution to *Four Theories of the Press* summarises his views about the imperative need to 'shift away from pure libertarianism' (Peterson 1956: 73) and develop a news sense of responsibility for the media:

> Whether or not one agrees with the Commission, however, one conclusion is abundantly evident—pure Libertarian theory is obsolescent, as the press as a whole has in fact recognized. Taking its place is an emerging theory which puts increasing emphasis on the responsibilities of the press, although it is still too early to discern what the full-blown form of theory will be. Individuals who still speak of freedom of the press as purely personal right are diminishing breed, lonely and anachronistic.

There is, quite surprisingly, a fourth mastermind behind *Four Theories of the Press*: Jay Jensen (Nerone 1995: 16–17). By the time the book was published (1956), Jensen was finishing his doctoral dissertation *Liberalism, Democracy and the Mass Media* at the University of Illinois. Jensen became part of the Illinois faculty, and eventually head of its journalism department. Great part of his work on the late 1950s and early 1960s focused on the analysis of the ideas behind the material causes imprinted on diverse communication outlets. That is, Jensen was interested on a detailed understanding of the ideology, discourse, comprehensive believes and ideas about the purpose and functioning of mass communication around the world. His argument was that different understandings (worldviews) about the legal, cultural, political function of the press, as well as its history, generate different media systems. In *Four Theories of the Press*' terms: 'the differences in the press of different countries reflect simply what people in different places and what their experience leads them to read about' (Siebert *et al.* 1956: 1).

Nevertheless, Jensen's concept of 'worldviews', in sharp contrast to Sierbert, Peterson and Schramm's uses of the term 'theory', aims at describing a specific, concrete and clearly identified historic period. 'One of the tensions that makes *Four Theories* interesting (and bedevilling)', condemns Nerone (1995: 17), 'is the unacknowledged discord between history and theory' (see below).

To sum up, *Four Theories of the Press* is a product of its time and of its authors' beliefs (Nerone 1995: 8). It started as a joint enterprise between scholars (the writers) and conservative businessmen (the sponsors) who aimed at counterbalancing general thinking about the media's goals and growing influence (especially the rise of television as a social force supplanting other agencies of socialisation, as well as the concentration of media ownership, threatening diversity and independence of viewpoints) in a bipolar world. As such, the book's premises and flaws are in great part a reflection of the historical period in which it was written, as well as each author's specific standpoints to understand and explain the interaction between political regimes and the mass media.

The 'Fantastic' Four

What with the years turned into the highly famous *Four Theories of the Press*, indeed emerged from two basic and contrasting '*philosophical and political rationales* or theories which lies behind different kinds of press' (Siebert *et al.* 1956: 2, emphasis added): authoritarianism and libertarianism. This might not come as a surprise if one keeps in mind, as described above, that the book is a product of the postwar years and as such, describes a world divided into two poles: the oppressed (ruled by authoritarian or communist regimes) and the free (enhanced by liberal democracies).

Four Theories of the Press offers thus a clear and brief explanation as to why these two different political and social settings (authoritarianism and libertarianism) produce different communication systems. The controls of the state and the restrictions that the ruling elites in authoritarian or communist regimes impose over the media produce a communications system that serves as a tool for the political regime: as part of the political process, mass media support and promote the regime's social and political objectives. A self-selected, unaccountable government, therefore, aims at monopolizing the control over information, public opinion and certainly the most useful, over citizens' political attitudes and social behaviour.

From this standpoint, a population aware and convinced of the power and legitimacy of its rulers will fully support an authoritarian regime and its policies or ultimate goals. A controlled media plays a crucial role in this process. 'An Authoritarian theory', writes Siebert (1956: 10), 'is a system under which the press [the media in general], as an institution, is controlled in its functions and operation by organized society through another institution, government'. This is how authoritarian rules control the social, political and economic structures through different means, including, of course, the media. Under this model of state-media relations, unaccountable and unconstrained political elites use mass media to pursue their own political objectives. It is the uncontested power of the state (or the government) that ensures its dominance over public communication by carefully organising and disseminating highly selective information through a 'puppet media' (Gunther *et al.* 1995: 4).

In this line of reasoning, the Soviet Communist theory is a development of authoritarian control systems. 'But because the Soviets have produced something so spectacularly different from older authoritarianism, and something so important to the world today', the authors specify (Siebert *et al.* 1956: 2), it was necessary to discuss some 'contemporary applications' (Siebert 1956: 27) and instruments for controlling the mass media. From this stance, two key differences emerge between authoritarianism and Soviet communism. First, under communism, the communicative power of the media represents a central piece for the regime's adequate functioning. It is the regime who has the duty, but also the responsibility of informing and guiding the public in achieving the common good. In other words, the communication objectives, processes and messages are determined by the Communist party, rather than generated in the (quite utopian) public sphere or imposed by the market. Second, a Communist rule has a complete monopoly as owners, investors, designers, directors and distributors of mass communication. That is, instead of leaving all (or most of the) channels of communication in the hands of private interests, it is the Communist party who, in the name of citizens, own, operate, invest on and directly distribute mass communication according to the aims and process embedded on a world revolution.

In sharp contrast, Siebert *et al.*'s 'Libertarian' and 'Social Responsibility' models of state-media relations describe a looser impact of the political regime over the media. In these models the latter are depicted as key guarantors of accountability and as effective surveillance mechanisms over the former. And even when democratic theory does not directly address the role of the media in these societies (see for instance: Scammell and Semetko 2000b), mass media are expected to keep citizens informed, ensure the free flow of political information, and enhance freedom of speech and assembly by giving voice to a wide range of actors and by opening the public debate to diverse viewpoints.

Additionally, constitutional rights or social conventions protect the media from potential arbitrary powers of governing elites, the state or the market.

Specific legal frameworks shield the media against political controls ensuring a free access to information and diversity on the ownership of media outlets. The essential function of these regulations is to guarantee that mass media remain free from unrestricted governmental controls, state domination or market manipulation, so that they are able to pose strict checks and balances over the political regime.

For the 'Libertarian' model of state-media relations, a healthy and independent economy becomes essential in being able to support the media as an industry of information and entertainment. Advertising and other commercial revenues thus become key sources of economic support that ensure the media's well-functioning and independence from government influence or even domination. The principal function of the political regime under this model is then to provide the bases for stable economy and strong legal frameworks that protect and promote the free development of the media as a commercial entity.

For the 'Social Responsibility' model, however, the media also have the moral responsibility of ensuring the right to information: the media should be 'accurate; it must not lie [. . . and it] must identify fact as fact and opinion as opinion' (Peterson 1956: 87). Hence, the state 'must not merely allow freedom; it must also actively promote it [. . .] it may enact legislation to forbid flagrant abuses of the press which poison the wells of public opinion, for example, or it may enter the field of communication to supplement existing media' (p. 95). Thus, in a socially responsible media system, the state should intervene, albeit cautiously, in the functioning of the media to ensure that they fulfil their tasks and duties. State intervention over the media may exist, but it would not be as heavy and perverse as it is under authoritarian or communist regimes and would be restricted to protect freedom of expression—even from the media themselves—as a cornerstone of political liberty.

The long-lasting influence of *Four Theories of the Press* can then be summarised into four key aspects: (1) its capacity to reflect the division of the Cold War (democracy *vs.* authoritarianism/communism) in explaining differences about the media's functioning around the world; (2) its normative approach to 'what media should be and do' stressing that freedom of expression (or press) as one of the fundamental functions of the media is a natural right that comes with certain responsibilities for the media; (3) its brevity and simplicity to set different models through the analysis of a manageable number of variables (such as historical time, philosophy, chief purpose, ownership and use of media, controls and regulations), and; last but not least (4) its tempting invitation to challenge its core assumptions.

How to Write a Best Seller

In pondering *Four Theories of the Press'* success against its flaws, Merrill (2002: 133) identifies 'maybe the secret formula' that made 'this formidable little book' a great sensation among scholars, students and practitioners. First, Merrill deduces, keep it short. In less than 150 pages, Siebert and his colleagues make the case for and explain differing normative paradigms about political philosophy, government accountability and scrutiny, freedom of expression, civic participation and public choice. 'Partly, the differences in the press of different countries', resolves the book (1956: 1), 'reflect simply what people do in different places and what their experience leads them to want to read about'.

Second, keep it simple. Actually, 'in simplest terms', reads its opening page (1956: 1), 'the question behind this book is, why is the press as it is?' Table 1.1 below depicts the book's main research question in relation to the other two that guided the authors' analysis. It also presents the book's

Table 1.1 Four Theories of the Press: Research Questions, Arguments and 'Theories'

Central research question:

Why is the press as it is?
'By *press* in this book we mean all the media of mass communication' (p. 1)

Complementary research questions:

Why do media of mass communication serve different purposes?
Why do they appear in widely different forms in different countries?
Why, for example, is the press of the Soviet Union so different from our own (U.S.), and the press of
Argentina so different from that of Great Britain?
What are the philosophical and political rationales or theories which lie behind
    different kinds of press?

Thesis:

The press always takes on the form and colouration of the social and political structures within which it operates

Key arguments:

The mean of mass communication reflects the social system of control whereby the relations of individuals and institutions are adjusted
An understanding of these aspects of society is basic to any systemic understanding of the press
To see the differences between press systems in full perspective one must look at the social system in which the press function
To see the social systems in their true relationship to the press, one has to look at certain basic beliefs and assumptions which the society holds

(Continued)

Table 1.1 (Continued)

These beliefs are related to: the nature of the man; the nature of society and the state; the relation of man to the state, and the nature of knowledge and truth

The analysis of the differences between press systems in one of philosophy; the philosophical and political rationales or theories which lie behind the different kinds of press we have in the world

Theories of the press: Since the beginning of mass communication, in the *Renaissance*, there have been only *two or four* basic theories of the press according to how one counts them

Two	**Authoritarian.** Developed soon after the invention of the printing in the authoritarian climate of monarchies' absolutism (16th and 17th centuries). Though not necessary government-owned, media is assumed servant of the state with the main purpose of supporting political elites
	Libertarian. As product of the *Enlightenment*, media are conceived partners in searching the truth: their main purpose is to serve as check and balances of the political power. Freedom from the government is thus imperative, as well as free access to ideas and information. Media's additional functions in the society are to inform, entertain and sell
Four	**Soviet Communist.** Modern (20th century); a development of the *Authoritarian* theory. Grounded on Marxism, the press is owned, directed and operated by the ruling party. Its chief purpose is to contribute to the success of the Soviet socialist system, especially the party in power
	Social Responsibility. Modification of the *Libertarian* theory (from 1950s onwards) as a response to the demands imposed over mass media in terms of responsibility, competition, diversity, access to information and fair representation

Source: Siebert *et al.* (1956: 1–7)

hypothesis and key arguments. As compact as this visual representation of *Four Theories of the Press* might seem, Siebert and his colleagues managed to pull all these ideas together in less than four paragraphs (pp. 1–2).

'It's easy to see why the book was initially successful', assents Nerone (2002: 135): 'it's short, it's readable, it's easily plugged into a course that belongs in every j-school curriculum, and it talks confidently about big issues'. Siebert and his colleagues actually explain these 'big issues' parsimonious, direct and clearly in just few lines that might serve as summary of the book:

> media reflect the system of social control whereby the relations of individuals and institutions are adjusted [. . .] An understanding of these aspects of the society is basic to any systematic understanding of the press.
>
> (1–2)

From this perspective, *Four Theories of the Press*, adds Nerone (*ibid*), 'is a wonderful gift for students struggling to understand how a complicated world is *supposed* to operate' (original emphasis). And this is precisely how the book becomes a handful teaching tool that students actually like (Nerone 2004; Merrill 2002). The study of the media in a historical context is not an easy task. History is complex and a great part of that complexity appear worthless to young students. *Four Theories of the Press* instead provides a set of ideal-types (although the authors do not recognise or label them as such) for organising different media systems around the world. It does it not act as a substitute for a complex history of mass media or for intricate philosophies around media systems, but as a toolbox for evaluating and explaining some pieces of these differing media 'theories'.

Third and closely related to the previous point, for a book to be just as appealing to academics than to practitioners or students it should be descriptive and neatly organised (Merrill 2002). In the case of *Four Theories of the Press:* an introduction; four short chapters with provocative subtitles and definitely no discussion or conclusion. Siebert and his colleagues put forth a typology of media systems that is explained using historical but brief reviews of authoritarianism, liberal democracy, communism and social responsibility as contrasting political rationales that shape the way citizens and their governments rely (or not) on their corresponding means of mass communication. As said, the authors confidence on describing the world in such brevity and simplicity gives students the parsimony they need to organise their knowledge and ideas. They might be different ways to understand and to explain divergent political regimes, and therefore alternative typologies of media systems might emerge (see below). But that is precisely one of the assets for bringing *Four Theories of the Press* into a classroom: it serves to organise the history and philosophy behind media systems at the same time that it generates suspicion, debate and ample criticism (Nerone 2002).

Fourth, 'give it a good, clear title that is riding the waves of popularity at the time of publication' (Merrill 2002: 133): *Four Theories of the Press: the authoritarian, libertarian,* social responsibility *and* soviet communist *concepts of what the press* should be and do (emphasis added). Much has been written about how the authors (perhaps purposely) misused the term 'theory' (see below). But the book's title is an invitation to learn more about what the press is, but possibly more intriguing (and problematic), what the media *should be*; a suggestion that even (more) today it is difficult to uphold with such boldness.

Fifth, make sure the book uses 'economy in words and price (be sure it's in paperback)' (Merrill 2002: 133), or for the current digital deluge, be sure it is an ebook. *Four Theories of the Press* is among the all-time bestsellers of the University of Illinois Press (Nerone 2002: 135). No other compilation on comparative media politics has sold so many copies; has been translated into so many languages, and has become a reference for graduate and postgraduate courses on almost any course on media and politics, journalism, international communication and mass communication in general (Nordenstreng 1997: 97). Plus, in this era of digital access and promiscuous pdf files, one can easily get access to *Four Theories of the Press*. A recent google search (April 2017) using the books' title showed more than 5 million results in 0.37 seconds. Plus, almost any library that holds a communications section has got a copy. For a 'horror-movie zombie for decades beyond its natural lifetime' (Hallin and Mancini 2004a: 9) or a 'classic [that] is already a museum piece' (Nordenstreng 1997: 97), the book remains very much alive, making its main premises and arguments easily accessible for (and dubious to) anyone interested on media systems.

Pitfalls, Lapses and Complaints: What *Four Theories of the Press* Should Have Been and Done

For more than sixty years now, *Four Theories of the Press* has been both enormously influential (Hachten 1981; McQuail 1983; Altschull 1984; Picard 1985; Hallin and Mancini 2004a) and widely attacked (for summaries see: Nerone 1995; Servaes and Lie 1997; Christians *et al.* 2009). When academics, for instance, have turned from the book's underlying normative assumptions to more detailed records of experience, the theoretical frameworks and the normativity proposed dramatically clash with the actual functioning, structure and performance of both political regimes and media systems.

As a matter of fact, complaints over *Four Theories of the Press* are fairly obvious and, frankly, quite redundant. First, there are naturally, hearty (and extremely well-sustained) protests about the rather confounding use of the term 'theory'. Put it shortly, the construction of role models or theoretical frameworks without testing them outside classrooms or libraries is an academic practice that could hardly be called 'theory'. In a later work, when reefing to media systems, Schramm (Rivers and Schramm 1969) replaced the word 'theory' for 'concepts'. It might be the case that the authors decided to use the former over the latter in the groundbreaking study not because they were particularly cautious (or extremely worried) about the scientific foundations or the academic rigour behind their theories schema. But because 'in those years', writes Merrill (2002: 133), '['theory'] was a term that implied scholarship, intellectual content and significant conceptualization' [. . .]. "Four Systems of the Press" would not do. "Four Perspectives on the Press" would not do. But, "theories", yes by all means'. Perhaps, he (Merrill 2002; Nerone 2002) adds, one of the reasons why the book has continued to work for so long is the slipperiness around the use of the term 'theory': it can mean different things for different people at different times.

Second, the question arises as to what exactly were Siebert, Peterson and Schramm counting (Nerone 2004: 29). The confusion is naturally bounded to the previous point on what exactly a 'theory of the press' is (or *should* be). On one level, the term seems to be referring to divergent philosophies (doctrines) about the nature of the truth and knowledge as cornerstones of any media system. On another level, 'theory' seems to indicate differing 'worldviews' as in Jensen's work. On yet an additional level, the terms points at particular institutional frameworks and ideologies behind the structure and functioning of mass communication. Nevertheless, as obvious as it might seem, communication 'theories' are not the same as communication 'systems'. But *Four Theories of the Press* seems indifferent to this crucial discrepancy. In their description about contrasting political philosophies that guided diverse historical mass communication periods in different parts of the world, Siebert, Peterson and Schramm keep referring to media 'theories' when they were actually describing media 'systems'. The opening pages of the of the book uphold (1956: 2):

> To see the differences between *press systems* in full respective, then, one most look at the *social systems* in their true relationship to the press. To see the social systems in their true relationship to the press, one has to look at certain *beliefs* and *assumptions* which society holds; the nature of man, the nature of society and the state; the relation of man to the state, and the nature of knowledge and truth. Thus, in the last analysis the difference between press *systems* is one of *philosophy*, and this book is about the *philosophical* and political *rationales* or *theories* which lie behind the different kinds of the press we have in the world.
>
> (emphasis added)

These fundamental lines might have solved the confusions created around a(n apparent) random and inadequate use of the term 'theory'. As mentioned before, *Four Theories of the Press'* key argument (perhaps theory, but only one) is, borrowing Nerone's (1995: 18) words 'that in structure, policy and behaviour the *communications system* reflects the society in which it operates and in which society can be categorically defined by a coherent *philosophy* (emphasis added). Or in Siebert and his colleagues (1956: 1) word's: 'the press always takes on the form and coloration of the social and political structure within it operates'. Clear and simple. But once and again, *Four Theories of the Press* uses the term 'theory' the same way, referring rather to social or press systems, than to philosophies, rationales, ideologies, traditions, practices or a set of belief, assumptions and values.

Putting aside the (unsolved) tension around term 'theory', a third key questioning is about the number of theories purposed. As argued in the previous paragraph, *Four Theories of the Press* seems to put forth only one 'theory': different social and political systems yield different media systems. That is, what the book actually does is to present different examples (perhaps grouped into four ideal types) of diverse philosophies that sustain contrasting social systems and their corresponding communication systems. For others, however, the 'Four theories' are actually only two: the authoritarian and the libertarian. As said before, Siebert, Peterson and Schramm are clear about this point. For the authors, the Soviet Communist and the Social Responsibility the theories are correspondingly developments of the Authoritarian and the Libertarian (p. 2). But the book loses sight of this distinction when it introduces, explains and describes the four theories. That is, as it is actually shown in a table (p. 7) that graphically summarises the four theories (context, history, purpose, ownership, means of control and key differences), all of them are treated at the same level and as such, no distinction is clearly made among them. This standardisation of media theories is even more surprising when one brings to mind that the book started as a research project on the social responsibility of the media (see above) and as such, the corresponding theory is indeed the main proposal and thus the real core of the book.

From an alternative standpoint, 'four' theories (or models) is too few and are actually not enough to describe a universal schema in which any media system neatly fits within a single category. In other words, it is just impossible to pack the whole world into a handful of and clearly distinctive fixed typologies. *Four Theories of the Press* actually imposes a simplistic 'ethnocentric perspective' (Merrill 2002: 133) pictured basically by a confrontation between the free (liberal democracies) and the oppressed (authoritarian rules): the West *vs.* the East.

Proliferation of Models

In looking for alternative approaches to overcome *Four Theories of the Press'* drawbacks, academics have tirelessly tried to adjust and modify the 'theories' proposed. Table 1.2 below shows key developments. As can be seen, moderate changes have included for instance, re-naming Sierbet *et al.*'s original concepts so that the new labels better describe (or highlight) political and economic developments of the time. More radical approaches have added new categories (McQuail 1983; Altschull 1984; Picard 1985), variables (Servaes and Lie 1997) or diverse levels of analysis (Hallin and Mancini 2004a). Others have engaged in a whole different enterprise, rejecting the original ideal-type categorizations by proposing more dynamic models to study the state-media relationship (Nerone 1995; Nordenstreng 1997; Christians *et al.* 2009) or putting forth alternative approaches to

Table 1.2 Different Models of the State-Media Relation Based on *Four Theories of the Press*

Siebert et al.	1956		Authoritarian	Soviet Communism	Libertarian	Social Responsibility	Additional Concepts
Author(s)	*Year*	*Title*	Concepts based on the four original categories				
			Authoritarian tending		Libertarian tending		Indeterminate tendencies
Williams	1967	*Communications*	Authoritarian	Paternal	Democratic		Commercial
Merrill and Lowenstein	1979	*Media, messages and men*	Authoritarian	Social authoritarian / Social centralist	Libertarian	Social libertarian	
Hachten	1981	*The world news prism*	Authoritarian	Communism	Western		Development Third World / Revolutionary
Martin and Chaudhary	1983	*Comparative mass media systems*	Communist		Western		Third World
McQuail	1983	*Mass communication theory*	Soviet communism		Libertarian	Social responsibility	Democratic participatory / Development communication
Altschull	1984	*Agents of power*	Marxists or communitarian		Market or Western		Advancing or developing
Picard	1985	*The press and the decline of democracy*	Authoritarian	Soviet communism	Libertarian	Social responsibility	Democratic socialists / Revolutionary

(*Continued*)

Table 1.2 (Continued)

Siebert et al.	1956	Four Theories of the Press	Authoritarian	Soviet Communism	Libertarian	Social Responsibility	Additional Concepts
Author(s)	Year	Title	Concepts based on the four original categories				Additional Concepts
			Authoritarian tending	Authoritarian tending	Libertarian tending	Libertarian tending	Indeterminate tendencies
Nerone	1995	Last rights	When the communist world collapsed, the corresponding media models were no longer functional and therefore replaced by different attempts to fit new democracies into traditional pigeonhole categorisations. Researchers, however, tend to conclude that the analysis of media systems emerging from authoritarianism require alternative theoretical lenses*				Alternative approaches to study media systems in democracies
							Questions *Four Theories'* actual capacity to explain the press-media relation due to its reliance on the classical liberal paradigm which has shown serious limitations to assess the role of the media even in old democracies
Servaes and Lie	1997	Media and politics in transition					Proposes a 'hermeneutic-interpretative' approach to the study of communication and socio-cultural change that takes into consideration aspects of power, ideology and culture
Hallin and Mancini	2004	Comparing media systems			Liberal model	Democratic corporatist model	Polarised pluralistic model
Christians et al.	2009	Normative theories of the media					Puts forward four roles to analyse the role of journalism in democracy: (1) monitorial; (2) facilitative; (3) radical; and; (4) collaborative

* See for instance: de Smaele (1999); Nordenstreng (1999); Ostini and Fung (2002); McNair (2005); Huang (2006); Sparks (2008); Gunaratne (2010); Hallin and Mancini (2012); and Voltmer (2012)

depict different political and social realities around the world (Nordenstreng 1999; Ostini and Fung 2002; Gunaratne 2010; Chengju 2006; Sparks 2008; Hallin and Mancini 2012; Voltmer 2013a).

Hanitzsch (2008) suggests four historical stages to describe the main developments of academic research on media systems that are useful here to organise these (at times confusing and quite repetitive) typologies. The first stage, the 1950 to mid-1960s, portrays the 'U.S. and the rest' (p. 113). This is, during these years researchers concentrated on the study of the U.S. and, from there, draw general (frequently contested) conclusions about the rest of the world, understood basically as 'the others'. *Four Theories of the Press* is an icon of this era: an U.S.-centrism embedded on a modern West (the U.S. and Western Europe) that clashes with the traditional East (Eastern Europe and the USSR); a political biased view of a world divided in two geopolitical blocks. In the context of the Cold War, each block seeks to impose its particular understandings about the role, functioning and uses of mass communication. The 'rest' (Africa, Latin America or Asia) actually does not appear in the analysis under a tacit understanding that one of the two blocks (democracy or communism) might eventually lead the Third World.

During a second stage, mid-1960s to early 1980s, research depicts the contrast between 'the North and the South' (Hanitzsch 2008: 114). It is at the height of the Cold War when researchers seem to admit that media systems typologies cannot exclusively be described as the industrial North, practically ignoring the underdeveloped global South. At that time, something interesting was actually happening in the Third World in terms of politics and the media: mass communication seemed to the potential to be used as a tool for development; or in contrast, it might had been turned into a potential weapon of manipulation and propaganda. The works of Williams (1966 /1962); Merrill and Lowenstein (1979); and Hachten (1981) fit on this trend.

Raymond Williams, for instance, put forth a typology also comprised of four communication systems (Williams 1966), but labeled slightly differently: (1) authoritarian, mirroring Siebert's (1956) description to the Authoritarian theory; (2) paternal, an authoritarian system with a certain conscience and respect for mass communication; (3) commercial, run by supply and demand forces; (4) democratic, a public broadcasting service free from the controls of the state or the market. As with *Four Theories of the Press*, a neat classification of media models serves to propagate the idea of different media systems according to divergent political philosophies. European philosophers and scholars such as Habermas (2006); Curran (1991); Keane (1991); or Garnham (1990) cultivated the concept of democratic media system that from very diverse standpoints assesses the need and the primary objectives of mass communication for democracy to take roots (Norden-streng 1997).

As shown in Table 1.2, Merrill and Lowenstein (1979) also proposed a typology drawing on (but mainly as a critique of) *Four Theories of the Press*. Focusing on mass communication ownership (by the state or by private business groups), the authors kept the Authoritarian model to put special emphasis on the negative consequences of state controls over mass communication such as repression, underdevelopment, manipulation or cohesion. They also kept the Libertarian model to depict a media system completely free from the controls of the state, but subject to the rules (and dangers) of the market. The two additional media models use the 'social' prefix (as in the original Social Responsibility model) to put emphasis on the kind of controls over the media that aim at benefiting the public. These models are: the 'social-libertarian', assuming minimal but positive state controls; and the 'social-centralist' (but renamed 'social-authoritarian' in a second edition of *Media, Messages and Men*), a label that originally pursued two goals: (1) to remove potentially damaging Cold War connotations by differentiating communism—which in principle uses mass communication media to propagate world revolution (Schramm 1956)—from the drawbacks of despotic authoritarian rules (dictatorships, military, single-party or totalitarianism), and; (2) to build a conceptual bridge between socialism and Peterson's (1956) notion of social responsibility (Ostini and Fung 2002).

Hachten's *The World's News Prism* (1981) is also inspired by the need of reconsidering the idea of mass media described by the free *vs.* the oppressed. The author also uses a five typology to picture a world were mass communication responded to different political and economic interests. He (Hatchen) retained the authoritarian and communist concepts, but merged the libertarian and social responsibility into an overall category labeled 'Western'. The name implied that in this region of the world, media were relatively free from arbitrary government controls. Trying to expand the analysis from the recurrent Northern pole, the author introduced two additional categories: the revolutionary and the developmental. The former tried to depict a media system committed to (illegal and subversively) challenging the unlimited power of authoritarian regimes, while the latter recognised the 'Third World' as completely different political and economic scenarios where media had to adjust their structure and functioning to each country's characteristics. With the collapse of the communist rule in Eastern Europe, a third edition of the book (Hachten 1992) returned to a four-category typology that is different to the original *Four Theories of the Press* especially in the need of recognising the crucial differences between the global North and the global South. Critiques have pointed out that Hatchen's models (first with five typologies, later with only four) actually mix up two different kind of analysis of mass communication media: one that is defined by the kind of controls imposed by the state—authoritarian, Western, communist—, and the other by the functions of the media—revolutionary and developmental (Ostini and Fung 2002).

Martin and Chaudhary's *Comparative Mass Media System* and McQuail's *Mass Communication Theory* (both 1983) became useful textbooks in the study of mass communication. Both volumes tried to imprint a worldwide perspective on the analysis of media systems. In this endeavour, the contrast between the West and East was thus useful not only for describing divergent mechanisms of state control over the media—depicted on the communist *vs.* the Western or Libertarian models—, but also for explaining two different conceptions about the goals and uses of mass communication. As such, the two opposite political philosophies imprinted on *Four Theories of the Press* remain: authoritarianism *vs.* libertarianism. Furthermore, the comparison between the North and the South exemplify how these two competing 'theories' work beyond the traditional battery of the European case studies and the U.S. What emerges with more clarity in these two volumes than in previous works on media systems is that: (1) media is not a single noun, as *Four Theories* suggested when referring to *the press* for actually describing different mass communication outlets; (2) the actual structure and functioning of these heterogeneous mass communication outlets in most of the countries do not perfectly match a single category since all media outlets 'depict a mixture of several elements' (McQuail 1992: 133, quoted by Nordenstreng 1997: 103).

Altschull's typologies—Marxist or communitarian; market or Western; advancing or developing—also follow the analytical trend of the era. Nevertheless, his *Agents of Power* (1984, 1995 2nd ed.) focuses the analysis on the interests (public or commercial) that drive mass communication. His view is that media are instruments (agents) of those in (economic or political) power. In other words, divergent, ideological forces and practices might describe mass communication in each of Altschull's worlds (the West, the East, the developing). But something common to the media in general and to journalism in particular all over the globe is that media is unable to fulfil the functions imposed by liberal democratic paradigm: to inform, to entertain, to be financially independent—as Siebert (1956: 51) envisioned in *Four Theories of the Press*. Independence (be it described as freedom of expression, political diversity, financial autonomy, neutrality, political balance or social responsibility) emerges, thus, as a mere 'article of faith' (Altschull 1995: 427) and as such, it is not possible to use it as a parameter to evaluate the functioning of the media under divergent political regimes and social conditions.

From its part, looking at the functioning of socialism in Scandinavia— this is beyond the usual USSR and Eastern Europe perspectives—, Picard

(1985) introduces the notion of 'democratic socialist'. Added to the original *Four Theories*, this concept aims at analysing the intervention of the state on mass communication as a tool to protect (not to put at risk) the media as mechanisms to serve the people's ideas, interests or needs especially in terms of political participation and representation. The concept of 'democratic socialist' is an abstraction that naturally builds on the notion of social responsibility, but that tries to move on from a Cold War impasse that matches socialism to negative connotations such as control and repression.

All in all, works trying to adjust *Four Theories of the Press* to the political and economic realities of the Cold War's peak (1970s and 1980s)—from Merrill and Lowenstein (1979) to Picard (1985)—aimed at two main tasks: (1) to include a more detailed analysis of the developing world, thus the need to include categories such as revolutionary, advancing or developing; and, (2) to question the participation of the state on mass communication (as owner, designer or regulator) exclusively as a perverse and dangerous practice.

With the breakdown of the Soviet rule, the late 1980s and 1990s returned to a research dynamic described by Hanitzsch (2008: 113) as 'the West and the West' perspective. Building upon the Libertarian and the Social responsibility paradigms, this research tried to develop alternative normative media typologies or approaches (even perhaps theories in an effort for emulating Sierbert and his colleagues' boldness) able to depict the differences of media's structure and functioning especially among democracies, old and new. The works of Nerone (1995) and Servaes and Lie (1997) depicted in Table 1.2 (above) exemplify this effort. Nerone and his colleagues' *Last Rights* (1995) questions *Four Theories of the Press* for its liberal approach to mass communication. From different angles (media systems, journalism, international communication, to mention some), the Libertarian paradigm shows serious limitations to assess the role of the media even in old or well-established democracies. For instance, divergent media systems in Western Europe and the U.S. face different challenges in terms of freedom of expression, diversity, plurality and civic representation.

From its part, the volume edited by Jan Servaes and Rico Lie, *Media and Politics in Transition* (1997) proposes a 'hermeneutic-interpretative' approach for a study of mass communication and socio-cultural change that takes into consideration aspects of power, ideology and culture. This is, it is not just politics that have changed dramatically all over the world: in the East, with the fall of the Soviet rule; in the West, with changes on political parties, representation and political participation; in the global South, with the breakdown of authoritarian regimes and the rise of transitional democracies. But, mass communication has also seen some key transformations, especially in terms of emerging communication technologies, formats and platforms that give rise to some optimist (though inevitably cautious) calls for global access, connectivity and renewed political participation. The resulting scenario is a world with multiple cultures; disenchanted global and local citizens (the same in democracies, post-communists rules or transitional regimes); soundless, but costly political communication processes driven by entertainment and economic interests rather than by distinctive political goals and philosophies.

Naturally, trying to find new schemas for the study of media systems, especially moving on from the West *vs.* East (democracy *vs.* communism) paradigm imprinted by the Cold War is an understandable research development since the breakdown of communist rule made the corresponding model(s)—named for instance: Soviet Communist, Paternal or Social Authoritarian—obsolete or outdated categorisations. Nevertheless, what stands out from this stage of academic research on media systems is that the 'third wave of democratisation'[1] (Huntington 1991) did not have the same effect on the conceptualisation of the Authoritarian model (Nordenstreng 1999: 150; Becker 2004: 143). The fall of different authoritarian rules around the world made clear that these regimes were different from each other and posed dissimilar challenges (and opportunities) to democratic transitions (Linz and Stepan 1996b; Geddes 1999; Hadenius and Teorell 2006; Linz 2000; Diamond 2002; Levitsky and Way 2002). Nonetheless, the analysis of media systems kept trapped on the libertarianism *vs.* authoritarianism dichotomy imprinted on *Four Theories of the Press* even some decades before the pick of the Cold War, the end of the Soviet rule or the third wave of democratisation.

Partly as a response to this impasse that pictured the world as two opposing blocks—regarded as the West and the East; the global North and the global South (developed *vs.* developing), or; the West and the West (old and new democracies)—, the new century brought a renewed impulse for studies on 'the West and the global' (Hanitzsch 2008: 113). From this stance, the 2000s witnessed a growing interest for comparative research on media systems (see for instance: Park and Curran 2000; Gunther and Mughan 2000a; Hallin and Mancini 2004a; Esser and Pfetsch 2004; Livingstone 2012). In general terms, write Curran and Park (2000: 2), the goal was to react 'against the self-absorption and parochialism of much Wester media theory'. This is, to start questioning universal generalisations about the media based on evidence derived from a 'tiny handful of countries'.

The icon for this period is Hallin and Mancini's *Comparing Media Systems* (2004a). In what has also become a bestseller (but perhaps faster than *Four Theories of the Press*) for comparative media studies, the authors put forth three models of media and politics: the Mediterranean or Polarised Pluralism; the North/Central or Democratic Corporatist; the North Atlantic or Liberal. The divergences among these three (geographically arranged) media systems are marked by different political systems on the one hand (although all the eighteen countries analysed are democracies), and specific characteristics of the media on the other. Hallin and Mancini's political system variables draw on comparative politics and political sociology literature allowing different levels of analysis. These variables are, for instance, differences between political systems in terms of regulation (the development of a rational-legal authority) and representation (pluralism, consensus or majoritarian patterns of government).[2] On the other hand, their media-system characteristics address aspects of the structure of media markets (circulation rates, ownership, concentration); 'organisational connections' or 'institutional ties' between politicians (government officials, parties, trade unions) and media personnel (journalists, media owners, editors); partisanship of media outlets or audiences; professionalisation patterns or the development of a 'journalistic culture' (beliefs, norms and practices), and; the degree and nature of state intervention in the media (regulation, funding, source of public information).[3]

A fifth era labeled 'homogenisation and its critiques' might be added to Hanitzsch (2008) perioidisation. Inspired by (or perhaps as a critique of) the influential *Comparing Media Systems* (Hallin and Mancini 2004a) the 2010s are seeing an unparalleled academic effort for understanding and explaining the differences among media systems, especially beyond the already well-known battery of Western case studies. Thinking on the (low) quality and great diversity of democratic regimes around the world, research efforts brought by academics from very diverse backgrounds and nationalities contest the notion that all media systems are actually targeting to the Libertarian or the Social Responsibility ethos. The quality of the media might be a key indicator of democratic rules' strength: a responsible media enhances good democracy, as Siebert and his colleagues proposed more than a half century ago. But the reverse also applies and as such it is also relevant to investigate how the quality of democracy influences (mainly restricts) the role that media might play in the political process. The searchlight is thus moved from a Libertarian normative paradigm—or the Social Responsibility ideal type to which all media systems are targeting—to the structure, organisational dynamic, rulings and history of both the political regime and the media (see for instance: Gross and Jakubowicz 2013; Voltmer 2013a; Guerrero and Márquez-Ramírez 2014; Zielonka 2015).

Conclusions

Sixty years of studying (on these pages organised into five stages of developments on) media systems have rendered a large and diverse (at sometimes overwhelming and confusing) series of 'typologies that serve the purpose of analytical distinctions and not of totalizing labels' (Nordenstreng 1997: 108). As a matter of fact, no single political regime or media system fits easily into the different categories or normative models developed to build upon Siebert *et al*.'s work. It is beyond the scope of this book to debate the accuracy or flaws of these proposals. What here remains useful is to highlight the fact that most of the work done in the last few decades have focused on adapting or adding new concepts to explain the relationship between the state and the media in democracies (old, transitional or developing). Whether such an 'Authoritarian' or a 'Libertarian' model exists, have existed or can exist—especially when thinking about the Social Responsibility ideal type or Libertarian normative approaches to state-media relationships—is something that has increasingly concerned current research on the interaction of political regimes and media systems. To some extent, the view that the media in non-democratic regimes was (is) an instrument of the political regime, while in democracies the political regime becomes a healthy contributor of media's structure, functioning and performance has not only seemed simplistic to academics, but is also inaccurate. The next chapter of the book looks closely at the challenges imposed over the study of media systems by a view of a world sharply divided by authoritarianism (control) or democracy (freedom) (Mughan and Gunther 2000: 3–4).

Notes

1. As Huntington (1997: 3) puts it: 'the first, long wave of democratization that began in the early nineteenth century led to the triumph of democracy in some thirty countries by 1920. Renewed authoritarianism and the rise of fascism in the 1920s and 1930s reduced the number of democracies in the world to about a dozen by 1942. The second short wave of democratization after the WWII again increased the number of democracies in the world to somewhat over thirty, but this too was followed by the collapse of democracy in many of these countries. The third wave of democratization that began in Portugal has seen democratization occur much faster and on a scale far surpassing that of the previous two waves [. . .] This dramatic growth of democracy in such a short time is, without doubt, one of the most spectacular and important political changes in human history'.
2. Drawing on comparative politics and political sociology literature, Hallin and Mancini (2004a: 65) propose five principal political variables relevant to the comparative analysis of media systems. These are: 'the relation of state and society, and particularly the distinction between liberal and welfare-state democracy; the distinction between consensus and majoritarian government; the distinction, related to consensus and majoritarian patterns of government, between organized pluralism or corporatism, and liberal pluralism; the development of rational-legal authority; the distinction between moderate and polarized pluralism'.

3. The exact 'four major dimensions to which' according to Hallin and Mancini (2004a: 21), 'media systems in Europe and North America can usefully be compared' are: (1) the development of media markets, with particular emphasis on the strong or weak development of a mass circulation press; (2) political parallelism; that is the degree and nature of the links between the media and political parties; (3) the development of journalistic professionalism; and (4) the degree and nature of state intervention in media systems.

2 Beyond the Dichotomy
Authoritarianism vs. Democracy

Of course, it needs to be kept in mind that we are talking here about perceptions of the purpose of the press. As with all institutions, the practice is quite different from the theory [. . . The] taxonomy outlined here it is itself fictional, a suspension in space of that which is always in motion. It is a static representation of the dynamic and hence itself illusory. Still, insofar as it contributes to understanding of the system as a whole, it serves a distinctly useful end.

Herbert Altschull, *Agents of Power* (1984)

Foreigners have long believed that the Mexican government controls the press through the sale of newsprint by a company the government owns. Are they right? Wrong. Foreigners have long believed that the Mexican government exercises an overwhelming power to suppress or publicize any news or opinion it wants. Are they right? Again wrong. Conclusion: There is a free press and freedom of expression in Mexico. Right? Once more, wrong.

Raymundo Riva Palacio, *A Culture of Collusion* (1997)

The influence of *Four Theories of the Press* on the study of politics and the media—especially on comparative communication research that aims at developing regional or even world-wide typologies—is undeniable. Hence the struggle to contend the statement that divergent political regimes give rise to different media systems. More than six decades of research makes it actually almost logic and self-evident: media's structure, purpose and functioning are deeply influenced by traits of the political regime in which they are embedded (Siebert *et al*. 1956: 1). From this stance and boldly reducing the ideal-type schema imposed by *Four Theories of the Press* to a polarity, democracies foster freedom of expression (strengthening the media); totalitarian regimes restrict it (weakening the media).

Perhaps, as argued on the previous pages of this book, this line of reasoning made relatively much more sense in a bipolar world where the distinction between authoritarian rules and democracies was axiomatic. Naturally, that kind of categorical cut among political regimes that served academics as a compass in the study the state-media relation is no longer accurate. Not just comparative government and politics research tends to depict authoritarianism and totalitarianism as rare (Hague *et al*. 2016: Ch. 4), but the 'third wave of democratization' was, according to Huntington (1997: 3), 'without doubt, one of the most spectacular and important changes in human history'.

To be fair to *Four Theories of the Press*, rather than being a simple exemplification of divergent media systems around the world or as a broad prescription for a libertarian normativity on mass communicators, it is a more open-ended invocation to question the connections between freedom of the media (as privately held companies) and freedom of expression. Hence the need to think about (and take some actions for) the social responsibility of the media. It is not that the book itself vowed on applying a constrained vision on normativity directly linked to libertarian standards and ideals that should be honoured regardless of historical or geographical contexts. But the construction of static typologies or ideal types of media systems has certainly been an open invitation to do so (Mancini 2008; Nerone 2012).

Politics and the media are today radically different from what Siebert and his colleagues studied sixty years ago and yet, a great amount of academic research keeps holding tie to the notion that divergent political regimes (nowadays apparently reduced to authoritarianism *vs*. democracy) yield different media systems. Key differences, as Siebert and his colleagues did point out six decades ago, also emerge among democracies and among authoritarian rules (see for instance: Hallin and Mancini 2012; Dyczok and Gaman-Golutvina 2009; Lugo-Ocando 2008). It is from this stance that the apparent (yet unintended) sharp-cut between freedom (democracy) and control (authoritarianism or totalitarianism) eternalised by a restrictive reading of *Four Theories of the Press* becomes less and less defendable.

This chapter shows how the usual dichotomy between authoritarian rules that repress the media and democracies that enhance plurality greatly differs from what actually happened and perhaps more interesting, is happening around the world. Certain challenges emerge when continually assessing the relation between political regimes and media systems against constrained notions of normativity. That is, the standards set by raw typologies of media systems divert from how politics and media relate, but also from how these two entities used to relate under non-democratic political regimes that nowadays seem to be the exception to an apparently worldwide democratic rule.

Using one of the most emblematic authoritarian rules in the world as an example, Mexico, the following pages show how neither Mexican authoritarianism nor the process of democratisation fit perfectly in the assumptions set by fixed typologies of media systems. That is, what the state-media relation was during the authoritarian rule and, after, what the transition to democracy *should be* (as proposed by Siebert and his colleagues) greatly differs from empirical evidence. Furthermore, by contrasting the Mexican case with other transitional democracies, what follows points to crucial divergences among media systems during both the authoritarian rule and the process of democratisation. Rather than engaging in a process of diagnosis about the current afflictions of the state-media relation in post-authoritarian regimes, these pages propose a critical analysis of the different aspects that shape this relationship. The chapter closes thus by putting forward some key reasons for searching alternative analytical perspectives. The proposal is to move forward from the authoritarian *vs.* libertarian state of mind. Sheltered behind the highly influential categorisation schema eternalised in *Four Theories of the Press*, this stance inevitably incites constrained notions of normativity on the study of media systems. As shown in the following pages, normative ideals, however, do not substitute understanding the actual functioning of current systems.

Challenges and Consequences of Approaching to the State-Media Relation From Rigid Typologies

What does it imply to address the state-media relation from categorisations similar to the ones presented in *Four Theories of the Press*? Box 2.1 below depicts the main challenges embedded on normative approaches to the state-media relation. Firstly, normative paradigms are an invitation to assess the state-media relation according to what is good (freedom of the press propelled by the media) against what is bad (repression from the state). That is, critically examining the interaction between the state and the media becomes a kind of measurement system that helps academics to allocate media systems in an apparent polarity that situates authoritarianism and libertarianism as opposites (Agee *et al.* 1994). In this task, the goal becomes thus not to describe *why* and *how* politics and media actually relate to each other, but above all to describe what the purpose and procedures of this interaction *should be* (Christians *et al.* 2009: vi; Siebert *et al.* 1956).

In other words, on thinking media systems as ideal types, prescribing stands over describing the interaction between politics and the media. It might thus not be a coincidence that in the last years, comparative communication research has been overwhelmingly worried by the shortcomings of political communication all over the world (Swanson 1992): neither democratic political regimes nor the media are fulfilling their duties in terms of freedom of expression and diversity of voices in the public debate.

**Box 2.1 Main Challenges Embedded on Normative
Approaches to the State-Media Relation**

• A normative stance privileges assessments about the role of the
media in politics according to *what* it should be, beyond analyses
about *how* it is.

• A liberal paradigm assumes media and politics as two independent actors.

• Clear cuts between Authoritarian and Libertarian models of state-
media relation hinder a great diversity of controls (in kind and
strength) that both the state and the media impose over mass
communication.

• Media's factual role in politics loses sight when normative principles such as press freedom, independence, freedom of expression or participation are taken for granted.

• A constrained notion of normativity loses sight of the need to
include both macro- and micro-level analyses able to depict the
role that structure and agency play in this interaction.

Secondly, from a constricted notion of normativity that confronts authoritarianism *vs.* democracy, research holds securely to an approach modelled
by the liberal-democratic paradigm in which the politics and the media are
depicted as two independent actors (Nordenstreng 1997). 'Classical liberalism assumes', writes Nerone (1995; quoted by Nordenstreng 1997: 98),
'that we have freedom of the press if we are free to discuss political matters in print without state supervision'. The state *should* not interfere with
individual freedom and political choice, whereas the media has the right to
pursue government accountability through information and public debate.
When academic research points at the collusion of interests or at the interdependence of practices between the state and the media, more common than
not these practices appear as obscure (although recurrent) flaws of certain
political regimes that fall short on fulling the expectations imposed by the
liberal-democratic paradigm (Scammell and Semetko 2000b). Interference
(be it from the state, the market or the media themselves) is also approached
with a certain halo of scepticism overlooking positive potential influences
that certain political regimes do impose over the structure, functioning
and performance of the media in some countries, especially in transitional

democracies (Randall 1998; Gunther and Mughan 2000a; Voltmer 2006: Ch. 14).

For instance, drawing on the past dangers imposed by authoritarian and totalitarian rules, the role of the state in transforming media and communications in transitional democracies constrains the analysis to a normative account in which the state-media relation in new democracies *should* be free from the intervention of the state and *should* remain open to different forms of expression, association and political participation. Nevertheless, in these countries, the media has been unable to enhance their democratic functions without the explicit support of the state in terms of public security or legislation (Waisbord 2007). For instance, the media's capacity to act as 'watchdog' or 'Fourth Estate' greatly depends on the degree to which other political actors—i.e., the governing elites, political parties or civic organisations—have fully abandoned authoritarian behaviours and attitudes (O'Donnell *et al*. 1986; Dahl 1989; Gunther *et al*. 1995; Linz and Stepan 1996a).

Thirdly, the dichotomy imposed by fixed typologies that make a clear cut between control (such as Siebert and his colleagues' Authoritarian and Soviet-Totalitarian theories) and freedom (the Libertarian and the Social Responsibility theories), hinder, however, a great diversity of controls (in kind and strength) that distinctive political rules (authoritarianism but also democracies) do impose over the media beyond the broad conceptualisation of strict and perverse control or, in contrast, emancipatory freedom. As it will be shown in more detail in the following section of this chapter, even within one of the most emblematic authoritarian rules in the world, media did retain ample room for expansion so they became the buoyant commercial enterprises they are today. That is, political control and repression over the media was neither unlimited nor a guarantee of permanency for this (and almost any) authoritarian rule. Actually, at a certain point the media even played a key role in breaking down authoritarianism serving as a promoter of new ideas, a forum for public debate and dissidence or as a powerful industry. Furthermore, in democracies (old and new) the media also play a key role (although not always positive). Research has shown that control and repression are not capabilities privative to the state. The media also have their own channels and mechanisms to restrain information or to manage public debate according to their particular commercial, strategic or political interests (Wynn 2017; Dwyer 2016, 2015; Murdock and Golding 2016).

Fourth, a normative approach to media systems also privileges analyses that point to clear distinctions between responsibilities (carried out by the state) and rights (attained by the media). From this stance, media's capacity to define (and reach or not) their own duties (goals) and procedures (functioning mechanisms) loses sight. For instance, focusing on key normative principles—such as independence, freedom of expression, participation and association—the study of mass communication in transitions to democracy have automatically been linked to the role of media as the main channel to promote civic engagement and public debate. That is, media are regarded as key providers of the information that fosters participation and decision-making; as fundamental critics of interference of the state into individual freedom; or as key promoters of public debate and civic participation. Thus, the underpinning conceptual consensus is that the media have a central role in democracies by keeping people informed about political affairs, by closely examining the exercise of power by the state or other political actors, and by opening the public debate to a diversity of voices (Gunther and Mughan 2000a; Scammell and Semetko 2000b; Bennett and Entman 2001; Street 2001; Graber 2003; Gans 2003; Curran 2005). Nevertheless, more common than not, media tend not to honour their rights and in some cases, they actually impose potential dangers over the healthy development of democratic regimes. Critiques to media's role in democracies (old or new) all over the world are grounded on hard evidence about unscrupulous conglomerates; concentrated markets; low quality contents; use of selective sources; manipulative agenda setting, for mentioning some practices that are against what media *should be*. (Doyle 2002; Altheide and Snow 1979).

Fifth, when approaching the form and functioning of the state-media relation as determinants (positive or negative) of democracies' healthy development, some normative approaches (especially the liberal-democratic) downplay the key role that individuals actually have in this interaction, while others (like the Social Responsibility model) overemphasise the judgments that individuals make and even assuming that the solution to structural problems rest in the ethical behaviour of professionals. That is, more common than not, the state and the media are approached either as monolithic actors creating a false image of internal homogeneity or, in contrast, as a set of individuals (politicians on one side, media representatives on the other) that have divergent goals, duties and even principles. Politics and the media, however, are naturally formed by diverse individuals (from the state: politicians, public servants, congress people; from the media: owners, anchorpersons, editors, journalists). None of these individuals (whether they are part of the state or the media) pursue identical goals or behave in the same manner. For starters, media is a plural noun that requires a differentiation between, for instance, traditional mass media and new platforms. Key questions arise thus, as for: what are the differences between traditional media or on-line journalists? Is political campaigning turning to new platforms to better position candidates? Are government representatives now blogging- or 'twittering'-dependent?

To sum up, restricting the study of the state-media relation to a constrained notion of normativity sheltered behind rigid categorisations of media systems possesses dangerous risks for comparative research. These threats range from assessing the role of the media in a political regime according to a set of ideal types that imply certain rights and duties without questioning how and why the media are (or not) honouring these principles, to analyses that overlook the great diversity of actors, individuals and mechanisms of interaction between the state and the media: two plural nouns that impose a false impression of harmony and homogeneity.

From this stance, academic research suffers at least in three ways when the study of the state-media relation is approached from a stance that tends to privilege analyses of the what this interaction should be over the how it should be or, perhaps most interesting, why it actually is the way it is (see Box 2.2 below). One, the main risk embedded on using the state-media relation as an indicator of democracies' health (arguably) might not be ending up with ideal types that rarely materialise. The real danger resides on not treating this measurement system as emancipatory instruments (Christians *et al.* 2009). That is, using comparative communication research to ratify the worrying state of political communication loses its purpose when it is not complemented by critical analyses on the causes and possibilities of improving these faults and shortcomings.

Box 2.2 Some Consequences of Studying the State-Media Relation as a Set of Norms and Values

- Shortage of critical analyses about the rationale and actual functioning of philosophical assumptions about the state-media relation
- Insufficient dialogue among complementary but seemingly alien areas of study such as: media sociology or political communication; research on statutory regulation processes, media self-regulation and governance
- Lack of comprehensive analytical frameworks that encourage comparative research to simultaneously look at diverse levels of analysis

---

Two, the utility of normative (ideal) accounts about how the interaction between the state-media relation should be above descriptive (accurate) analyses becomes less and less clear since both areas of research actually advance separately. Media sociology and (perhaps in less stance) political or government communication research do advance by analysing how these entities function on daily basis. From its part, media law and regulation (be it by the state or by the market) also advance through critical analyses on the challenges embedded on statutory regulatory processes, media ethics,

governance and self-regulation. In their efforts, however, both areas of studies rarely speak to each other. Description and evaluation are complements,
but current academic research on the state-media relation tends to favour
one or the other.

Three, in a soul-reaching effort, comparative research on the state-media
relation simultaneously advances through analyses that privilege macro-
level indicators over meso- or even micro-level studies. This is, comparative
research still finds it very difficult to operationalise analytical frameworks
that cover a broad range of aspects raging from individual roles or personal
ethics to independent variables notwithstanding systemic characteristics
such as industries' markets or commercial guidelines, national politics or
philosophical rationales.

The following pages of this chapter exemplify the challenges embedded in studying the state-media relation applying fixed categorisations or
exclusively normative stances. Using an emblematic authoritarian regime
as an example, Mexico, the next section of the chapter shows how this
rule nourished particular relations with the media making it very difficult
to describe the Mexican media system with concepts such as control and
repression. When turning the searchlight to democratic rules, the third section of the chapter shows how a normative stance prevents more critical
approaches to media systems' current faults especially in the study of transitional democracies.

Authoritarianism: An Almighty Force?

Authoritarianism in Mexico is an intriguing case study (see for instance:
Meyer 1995; Krauze 1997; Escobedo 2000; Reyna 2009; Ugalde 2012).
It not only differed from the traditional characteristics of other authoritarian rules in Latin America, such as long military dictatorships, sup-
pressed civil society, controlled media, censorship or highly repressive
media regulation. It also lasted longer than other dictatorships around the
world: from the late 1920s until the early 1980s, a single political party
(the PNR, *Partido Nacional Revolucionario* and its predecessor the PRI,
Partido Revolucionario Institucional) was able to dominate the political
landscape. It won every presidential election; retained the majority on
both chambers of the Congress for almost six decades[1] by allowing certain
but limited political pluralism; ruled in most of the federal states at both
regional and municipal level,[2] and; lead diverse corporate, professional
and civic organisations.

Key to the durability of this particular authoritarian rule yet rarely
recognised by academic research, were the subtle mechanisms of control
that the ruling party established with the media. Control over the media

was grounded on structural arrangements and practices that allowed governing elites to keep close surveillance over both print and broadcasting. Direct government censorship and repressive measures were very rare since a complex network of mechanisms of collusion with the political regime, rather than strict control, proved to be efficient in nurturing a pro-government and relatively docile media (Guerrero 2009). The state-media relation during the authoritarian Mexico was thus sustained more on interdependence than on censorship, intimidation, political elites' direct ownership or official repression (Lawson 2002: 26). Equally effective to keep the media at close complicity was a complex network of intertwined incentives and mutual benefits that were flexible enough for adapting to diverse political conditions and for responding differently to each medium's particular interests and capacity of influence (Fernández Christlieb 1982; Riva Palacio 1997; Lawson 2002: Ch. 3 and 4; Trejo Delarbre 2004a, 2004b; Sánchez Ruíz 2005; Guerrero 2009, 2010a).

For instance, the incentives that Mexican authoritarian rule endowed to print media owners and journalists in exchange for positive news coverage touched every aspect of the press' structure and functioning: its finances, sales, distribution, means of production, personnel and sources of information (Vaca 2015: Ch. 2). During those years, authoritarian surveillance over the press, as the Authoritarian or Totalitarian models of media systems suggest (see Siebert 1956), was indeed tight and strict. However, throughout the decades these mechanisms of control became essential traits of the newspapers and journalism in Mexico. As a consequence, it was difficult to recognise the state's influence and manipulation in what at first glance appeared as relatively autonomous newsrooms and profitable publications. Collusion instead of control benefited both the political regime and the press. The former ensured the support and positive news coverage it needed to legitimise its rule, while the latter was able to subsist throughout long decades of economic turmoil and low circulation rates.

Regarding broadcasting, the Mexican authoritarian rule applied a slightly different set of collusion mechanisms to keep broadcasters at close complicity. Similar to what happened with the press, the main goal remained to keep close links with the industry (owners and workers) so that it was possible to restrain broadcasters' influence in communicating politics. Nevertheless, since it is the state that has ultimate control over the spectrum and technology that make broadcasting possible, the authoritarian regime felt it was unnecessary to craft a very complex set of incentives similar to the one that it had been using towards the press. On the contrary, it was a quite simple strategy: concessions would be only granted to loyal supporters. Over the years, however, this practice turned quite complicated since broadcasters (commercial entrepreneurs) grew into powerful moguls determined to defend their own political and economic interests (Guerrero 2009: Ch. 2). The authoritarian regime had to therefore go back to nourishing a close relationship with broadcasters which was guided by its experience with the press. The strategy was then again carefully crafted according to the needs of a mutually beneficial relationship flexible enough for adapting to both the broadcasters' demands and the governing elites' needs in terms of legitimacy and political support.

This implied at least three strategic actions: (1) to provide broadcasters with the technical and economic support they needed for developing as profitable private firms; (2) to use statutory regulation as control mechanisms; (3) to grant radio and television frequencies only to pro-government entrepreneurs[3] (Vaca 2015: Ch. 2). Over decades, the different PRI administrations strengthened these mechanisms through a confluence of interests between broadcasting magnates and governing elites. The authoritarian regime ended up offering to broadcasters juicy incentives such as quasi-permanent concessions, market concentration, tax exemptions, technical support and lax regulatory measures. In exchange, broadcasters granted the legitimacy and political support the regime requested through positive and self-censored news coverage. This 'mutual exchange of support' (Guerrero 2009: 46) greatly diverts from the one-sided statutory mechanisms of control traditionally pictured in the Authoritarian model of state-media relationships (Siebert 1956). In addition, it also highlights the need to reconsider the possibilities of achieving the free, civic-oriented and mutually vigilant interaction pictured by the Libertarian model (*ibid*). Both models (the Authoritarian and the Libertarian) downplay the interest that the Mexican governing elites and the Mexican media have had on preserving the benefits that they have long received from each other.

In terms of public broadcasting, in contrast to other authoritarian rules around the world that regarded it as a cornerstone for media control and censorship, the authoritarian regime in Mexico simply considered a public service media system unnecessary. From time to time, different PRI administrations revived the idea of a public service broadcasting. These initiatives (often failed or unfinished attempts) were more a product of particular political contexts rather than a deliberate effort to promote state-media relationships closed to the one envisioned by Peterson (1956) in his Social Responsibility model. On the contrary, the random possibility of a regime's direct participation in broadcasting or a government's more active role in media policy served as a warning for media moguls. The state had ultimate control over the electromagnetic spectrum that made broadcasting possible. Authoritarian rule could have always chosen to nationalise media assets, just as what other Latin American dictatorships did to ensure complete control over mass communication. Aware of this latent risk, throughout the long decades of the authoritarian regime Mexican broadcasters had to constantly convince the governing elites about the benefits of a commercial media system tailored to the political regime's needs such as loyalty, political support through extensive positive news coverage, and a buoyant industry.

This brief recount of politics and the media during the authoritarian rule in Mexico serves as an example of the risks embedded on approaching the state-media relation from rigid categorisations. Matching the Mexican case with ideal types of media systems might lead to conclude—without being entirely wrong—that, as the Authoritarian model of the press submits, Mexican authoritarianism imposed solid systems of media control under which the media, as an institution, was controlled in its functioning and operation by the government (Siebert *et al.* 1956: 10). In a broad sense, this did happen in Mexico. But not as straightforward as it might seem at first glance. Instead of repression or top-down enforcement, media control was attained through a more horizontal and interdependent relationship grounded on mutual benefits and compromises. It involved a complex set of influential informal practices, interactions, norms and self-imposed codes of behaviour. This functioning allowed both the political regime and the media to advance their own objectives: for the state, political control; for the media, growth as profitable business. In the end, through long decades of authoritarian rule, the political regime and the media remained as close allies correspondingly profiting from less obvious, but perhaps more devious mechanisms of control over the means of communication.

The Mexican case is also useful in pointing out differences among authoritarian regimes. This might not come as a surprise, since Siebert and his colleagues did show certain historical and contextual differences between authoritarian rules (the British Tudor or the fascist Italy, for instance). Nevertheless, rigid typologies have created a notion of homogeneity among groups. For instance, at first glance the most similar cases to the Mexican authoritarianism are other Latin American totalitarian rules. Not only do these countries share cultural and historical traits, but also media in the region shows very similar characteristics especially in terms of their influence on politics and regarding the size of these conglomerates (see: Lugo-Ocando 2008; Waisbord 2013).

However, a closer look at different national cases reveals for instance that crucial divergences among Latin American media systems do arise from the type of control that authoritarian rules imposed over the media. These differences, as shown in Box 2.3 below, range from the benefits and privileges media moguls received from authoritarianism (Voltmer 2013a: Ch. 4 and 5), to the governing elites' perceptions about the media's role in politics (Waisbord 2000, 2007).

Box 2.3   Media Control: Key Divergences Among Authoritarian Rules Around the World

*   Media ownership
*   Type and strength of the mechanisms of control from the state
*   Governing elites' perceptions about the role of the media in politics

---

For example, in contrast to the Mexican case, the military dictatorships in Brazil, Argentina, Chile and Venezuela served as the main developers of the media as an industry. These authoritarian rules not just invested large amounts of economic and political resources to keep the media at close complicity (as the PRI did in Mexico), but they also were in charge of the industry's technological development according to the communications demands of those times.

In Brazil, Globo grew as a powerful media conglomerate, financed by the political regime, but largely unregulated and closely linked to political elites (Guedes-Bailey and Jambeiro Barbosa 2008; Matos 2012; Porto 2012). In Argentina, the military dictatorship directly managed the radio and television (at least during the late 1970s and early 1980s), and a strict control over the press was achieved through 'absolute surveillance' and repression (Liotti 2014: 101). In the case of the latter, however, press owners were granted with different incentives (lack of regulation or controlled media markets, for instance) that guaranteed business continuity and progress. During Pinochet's rule in Chile (1973–1990), a close relationship with print media owners and a savage market competition for broadcasters ensured the authoritarian rule an indirect, but still severe control over mass communication (Araya 2014). Venezuelan radio and television were born in the early 1930s and 1950s respectively, under military rules that closely follow their early developments. Few decades later (1970s), both industries grew disproportionally to other broadcasters in the region thanks to a national oil boom. Surveillance was then carried out by an overwhelming presence of powerful international media conglomerates in control of both media markets and contents (Bisbal 2007; Capriles 1976).

In contrast to the military dictatorships in Latin America, military rules in Africa did not have the economic resources or perhaps the strategic intention of keeping the media at close complicity. Censorship and repression were the main mechanisms for controlling the media during those years. Historically, African media has struggled against political turmoil, lack of continuous investment on technology and human resources. As with the press during the nineteenth century, the colonial powers developed a rudimentary broadcasting industry that was regarded as a mechanism for exporting media contents and news to these territories. The intention was far from transferring the know-how or at least the technology to start developing an indigenous system of mass communication. Just after their independence (early 1960s), a wave of military coups in the continent took control of the political power from the elected governments that had replaced the colonial rule. Repression, censorship, closure of newsrooms, seizure of publications were commonly used to suppress opposition to military rule. African media, especially the press, suffered greatly (and did fight back) under these dictatorships (White 2008; Ngara and Esebonu 2012).

The crucial divergences among authoritarian rules broadly outlined here point to the need for a better understanding of the ample range of mechanisms that different authoritarian rules used to keep the media controlled. This divergence among different historical periods and among national case studies is not just about strength or type (direct or indirect, for instance) of the control imposed over the media, but also regards different conceptions among authoritarian rules about media's role in politics: instrumentalist, semi-independent but without interference, interdependence or submission.

Admittedly, Siebert and his colleagues were not blind about crucial differences on how dictatorships around a world depicted by the confrontation between the West and the East kept the media under close surveillance. Hence the explicit distinction between authoritarianism and totalitarianism (Siebert 1956). As explained before, two are the fundamental discrepancies closely related to the kind of control that communism imposes over the media: (1) an assumption about media's crucial and positive for 'the accomplishment of a world revolution'; (2) the strict monopoly that the communist party enforced 'over all avenues of reaching the masses' (Siebert 1956: 27, 28 respectively). Soviet-totalitarianism had thus a very specific notion about the role of the media as a cornerstone of the political regime. The USSR collapsed and with it (apparently) also the need to keep the distinction between authoritarianism and totalitarianism in the analysis of the state-media relation. As Mughan and Gunther (2000: 3–4) put it:

> The traditional view has been that the media are schizophrenic in character and play contrasting roles in the establishment and maintenance of political order in authoritarian/totalitarian regimes and in democracies: the media have been depicted as manipulative and subversive of individual freedom and political choice in the former and as guarantors of political liberties and government accountability in the latter.

In other words, when current academic research approaches the state-media relation from a normative stance it (apparently) does not matter which state-press relationships model or 'theory' is chosen since political regimes all over the world (and it seems that in consequence, media systems also) are inclined to authoritarianism (control) or democracy (freedom). Nevertheless, as seen, authoritarianism cannot be regarded as a set of homogeneous mechanisms of control over the media. As a matter of fact, control itself is a term in need of more clarification regarding, (1) its historical context, since authoritarianism is far from being extinct, and; (2) the dictatorship under scrutiny, since Mexican authoritarianism cannot be approached with the same hypotheses as the ones emerging from the study of other twentieth-century Latin American, non-democratic rules or current authoritarian regimes in Asia and Middle East.

Similarly, transition from authoritarian or totalitarian rules cannot be approached as a progressive linear movement toward normative ideals embedded on media systems that draw on the Libertarian or the Social Responsibility models. Additional tools are needed to first understand *why* transitional democracies are commonly depicted as failed efforts to achieve the liberal model. Second, empirical rather than normative analyses are necessary to identify the considerable differences among these countries that explain why and, most interesting, *how* these political remiges are relating to the media. The next section of this chapter looks back to the Mexican example. It shows that media liberalisation was not just a by-product of democratisation, as a normative research on the state-media relationships would have expected. Aside from a broader political transformation, media opening in Mexico was driven by changes on editorial lines, economic conditions, market competition and, to a lesser extent, the opening of the political process to opposition parties (Lawson 2002; Hughes 2006; Guerrero 2009; McPherson 2010). In this process, Mexican media was not a causal factor in the process of democratisation.

Democracy: Freedom and Independence?

How does the process of democratisation influence the media and vice versa? Documenting the consequences that a change of political regime imposed over Mexican media or analysing the role that these media have had in democratising Mexico is a daunting task. In contrast to other dictatorships in Latin America, the authoritarian regime in Mexico did not end abruptly. It was rather a slow process of political liberalisation: erosion of the regime's legitimacy; the breakdown of an authoritarian political culture; the growth of opposition parties; a gradual mobilisation of civil society, and; electoral reforms driven by progressive changes in the economy and the society (see for instance: Silva-Herzong 1999: Part II; Merino 2003; Loaeza 2008). Malleable, as it was traditionally understood and managed during the long years of PRI rule, the state-media relationship steadily adapted to these changing conditions. In 2000, when for the first time in Mexican history an opposition party won a presidential election, Mexican media had, as Lawson (2002: 3) puts it: 'escaped, evaded, or resisted official control [. . .] and Mexico's Fourth Estate was [arguably] firmly established' (p. 91).

Contrary to what traditional models on state-media relationships anticipate (for instance, that media transformation is a by-product of broader liberalisation in the political system), the Mexican case shows first that the opening in the media was not solely the result of political pluralism, and second, that democratisation did not guarantee media diversity. Media liberalisation in the country was a result of changes on the market rather than a particular struggle for civic participation or pluralism in the public debate (Guerrero 2009, 2010b). This transformation has led to the concentration of media ownership, especially TV, on the few commercial groups that do not hesitate to use the prominent role of mass communication in politics to advance their own economic or political agendas (Trejo Delarbre and Vega 2011).

In this context, some academics see the opening of Mexican media (especially the press) as a detonator of crucial changes on public debate and civic participation (see for instance: Lawson 2002: Ch. 8; Wallis 2004; Woldenberg 2004). From this perspective, greater public awareness about government abuses (corruption, electoral fraud, repression, human rights violations, involvement in drug-trafficking) and radically different styles of reporting contributed to slowly eroding the legitimacy of authoritarian rule; propelled public scrutiny and forced the governing elites to respond to new demands in terms of public information and accountability.

However, a second strand of research stresses the internal and contextual challenges that the Mexican media faces in consolidating as a Fourth Estate (Hughes 2006, 2008; Guerrero 2009, 2010a; McPherson 2010, 2012). Along with other economic and social contextual factors (such as constant economic hazards, low literacy rates and a political culture that still privileges corporatist and paternalistic practices), market concentration and high entry costs for new competitors inhibit media pluralism and perpetuate authoritarian practices such as a dangerous degree of collaboration between politicians and the media.

For instance, Mexican broadcasting, especially television, keeps functioning under a strict concentration of the market through two commercial groups: Televisa and TV Azteca. These two networks control close to ninety-five percent of the television market in Mexico, making it the most concentrated media system in Latin America (Hughes 2006; Vidal 2008: Ch3). In the last decade, some key efforts had been made to open the market to new competitors. But high entry costs and incumbents' economic and political influence have made it very difficult to put an end to media concentration. Moreover, both companies (Televisa and TV Azteca) extend their influence to other commercial activities and financial conglomerates. To some extent, the cross-ownership and intricate financial networks shield the market from competition; an ingredient that, as seen in this chapter, proved to be crucial in breaking down the old establishment broadcasting system. Something similar happens regarding print media. Judging by the number and the diversity of publications at first glance, the Mexican press might appear to be open and competitive. Nevertheless, when it comes to newspapers of national circulation and consistent readership, the numbers of media outlets (and owners) come down again to few commercial groups of long-lasting tradition and strong presence in other commercial markets (Vidal 2008: Ch. 5).

Additional constraints for a vibrant Fourth Estate come from inside the media. More common than not, Mexican newsrooms struggle to overcome past authoritarian journalistic practices, archaic organisational structures and management strategies (Hughes 2006: Ch. 9; McPherson 2010: Ch. 4, 2012). As part of the long-lasting tradition of media conglomerates, some media owners, editors and journalists are still trapped in authoritarian assumptions or out-of-date mindsets. For instance, press and television newsrooms still fight against inertial corruptive practices such as compromising relationships with governing elites in exchange for information or even juicy advertising contracts. While some media owners and editors support more autonomous, assertive and politically diverse forms of journalism, others are still more concerned with high circulation rates and economic security (Trejo Delarbre 2004b; Bravo *et al.* 2011).

In face of these conditions, a third tract of literature critically assesses the actual capacity of Mexican media to translate the change of political regime into more accurate, professionalised and assertive journalism (Trejo Delarbre 2001; Sánchez Ruíz 2005; Guerrero 2010a; McPherson 2012). This approach sees media as an increasingly sophisticated mechanism of control that is capable of both enhancing civic participation and restraining it through political bias and market-oriented practices (Trejo Delarbre 2004a). From this stance, broadcasters for instance appear more open to plural and balanced news coverage, but at the same time, are keen to use their prominent role in mass communication to satisfy their own market goals and political agendas (García 2008: Part I, Ch. 3; Juárez 2009; Guerrero 2010a: 262–272). Thus, Mexican media moguls still prioritise their own particular interests such as financial and economic stability over a public or social commitment (Guerrero 2010b). Their watchdog activities, promotion of political competition or even the inclusion of other voices into the public debate are more appealing today than they were during the authoritarian regime not purely because democracy demands it, but because these practices also render high ratings and revenue figures (Guerrero 2009).

On balance, regardless the stance of academic research, Mexican media's form and functioning in the new political regime falls short of the expected performance in democracies. As growing comparative research proves, however, Mexico is not an exceptional case (see for instance: Randall 1998; Hydén *et al*. 2002; Romano and Bromley 2005; Voltmer 2006, 2013a; Lugo-Ocando 2008; Dyczok and Gaman-Golutvina 2009; Trappel and Meier 2011). Media all over the world, in old and new democracies, struggle to fulfil normative paradigms; the more research enquires there are about their theoretical origins and practical viability, the more academics hesitate to regard them as a list of requirements or guarantees for democracy and free media (Mughan and Gunther 2000; Park and Curran 2002: Ch8; Hallin and Mancini 2012).

Why does the state-media relation in transitional democracies diverge so greatly from the expectations imposed by the change of political regime? One of the key problems of bringing together the vast and varied amount of research on media and transitional democracies is the lack of a comprehensive framework for the analysis of the different aspects and ways of how democratisation influences the media and vice versa (White 2008). Not only is research on how democratic rules relate with the media dispersed among diverse areas of media studies (Canel and Voltmer 2014), making it difficult to apply a holistic theoretical approach addressing different aspects of this interaction. But also, this dispersed set of analytical tools have been created and tuned-up according to normative approaches developed mainly for the study of old democracies. Transitional democracies, however, do not fit neatly with 'Western media theory' (Park and Curran 2000: 3).

Hence, the vast (but dispersed) majority of the literature on transitional democracies tends to use the process of democratisation as an entry point for research. From this perspective, the state-media relation is expected to be transformed by a stronger and vigilant media that enhances accountability generation and pluralism in the public debate. From its part, the state is also presumed to abolish previous means of control (direct or indirect) over the media while it searches for alternative instruments to shield citizens from media concentration, manipulation or lack of journalistic professionalism. More common than not, this ideal scenario, however, clashes with what is really happening around the world.

Crucial divergences between the underlying standards of normative arguments about the state-media relation in divergent political regimes can be traced both into the past and the present. As seen, the preceding authoritarian rule imposes different challenges to the media in transition to democracy and to the consolidation process thereafter. Furthermore, political regime democracy has very diverse forms and meanings. This may seem an obvious point (see for instance: Dahl 1989; Geddes 1999; Held 2006), but much follows from it. It is not just the state-media relations in transitional democracies that face different challenges inherited by (potential) authoritarian legacies or path dependencies that prevent both the state and the media to change the course of this interaction and to fulfil the expectations imposed by the change from authoritarianism to democracy (see for instance: Gross 2002: Ch. 1; Ogundimu 2002; Lugo-Ocando 2008; Voltmer 2013a: Ch5). But the new democratically elected governments in these countries also have divergent understandings about how to put (or not to put) the liberal democratic paradigm into practice.

For instance, as seen, African democracies face enduring mechanisms of state control and an underdeveloped and frail indigenous media (Hydén *et al.* 2002; Blankson 2007; Kalyango 2011). In this scenario, a study of state-media relations that places special emphasis on empirical evidence (rather than on a pure normative approach to the role of the media in the democratisation process) helps to better understand *how* the state intervention and political control remains a key threat to democracy. This approach might be useful for unpacking the challenges African media face into a set of manageable empirical dimensions and for assessing their consequences beyond general assumptions of freedom *vs.* control, repression and censorship.

Latin American media also face different challenges. The resurgence of populism in some countries (Venezuela and Bolivia, for instance) has significantly marginalised the possibilities of a media modelled to the liberal paradigm. These political regimes have actually strengthened diverse control mechanisms that range from the expropriation of media companies to strict media regulation, disproportionate funding to government-led public media and sympathetic media owners (Lugo-Ocando 2008; Waisbord 2013). In a sharp contrast, purely commercial and powerful international media conglomerates (in countries like Mexico, Brazil or Colombia) also put democracy at danger. In this context, the greatest risks might not be state repression and control, but close-knit relationships between media moguls and political elites. During the consolidation process, both set of actors have appeared reluctant to lose the assurances and privileges gained through long decades of a controlled 'market place' of ideas. In fact, current research on the media in Latin American transitional democracies points at diverse range of factors explaining how and why the media are seriously struggling to fulfill the normative expectations imposed by the change from authoritarianism to democracy (for Mexico see: Lawson 2002; Hughes 2006; Guerrero 2009, 2010a; McPherson 2010, 2012; for Brazil: Albuquerque 2012; Matos 2008; for Colombia: Fox and Anzola 1998; Montoya-Londoño 2014).

Diverse studies have also pointed to crucial divergences among the media systems emerging in in the post-communism region of the world (for recent compilations see: Beumers *et al.* 2009; Dobek-Ostrowska *et al.* 2010; Downey and Mihelj 2012; Gross and Jakubowicz 2013). Here, the structure, function and operation of the media have without doubt dramatically changed. Nevertheless, the expectations of more freedom and independence in media performance clashes with other kind of economic and political aspirations. In Russia, for instance, the hierarchical and regional structure of the press have been replaced by a more horizontal non-political and local publications. A key motor in this process has not been the process of democratic consolidation, but of a rapidly growing advertising industry. Russian media dependence on business strategies—primarily advertising and entertainment contents—make them highly vulnerable since financial profits are closely related to informal connections between media entrepreneurs and politicians. Indirect influence of political elites and a growing commercialism are key characteristics of Russian media (Vartanova 2012). This close relation between media and political elites is also present in small states of South East Europe. In fact, in this region of the world, media's influence on domestic politics paints a different picture for the expected Europeanisation and media governance trends as (apparent) signs of democratic consolidation (Broughton-Micova 2013).

From this stand, democratisation appears more as a process rather than as the radical transformation pictured in the liberal democratic paradigm. It is a 'social experiment' (Voltmer 2006: 1) that requires a gradual adaptation to the new political conditions. The broad review of transitional democracies around the world presented in these pages shows three key elements that impose diverse challenges for the emerging state-media relation. As shown below in Box 2.4 these are: (1) the diversity of ways in which authoritarian legacies and path dependencies shape (constrain or enable) the state-media relation in the new democratic setting; (2) the influence of informal arrangements and practices in this interaction; and; (3) the interplay between change and stasis in the configuration of a new relationship between these two sets of actors. That is, an analysis that aims at critically assessing the current form and functioning of the state-media relation (instead of just pointing to its shortcomings according normative assumptions) might benefit from conceptual frameworks that take these aspects into consideration.

**Box 2.4 Beyond Normative Approaches to Media
Systems: Key Elements for the Study of
Transitional Democracies**

1. A diversity of influences in which the authoritarian past shaped the state-media relation in the new democratic setting
2. The influence of informal arrangements and practices in the state-media relation
3. An interplay between change and stasis

The argument is thus that the study of the state-media relation needs alternative conceptual and analytical frameworks able to unpack this interaction into different components such as history (legacies from the past); its capacity to change and adapt to the new political conditions; its actual functioning and its structure.

Conclusions

This chapter spoke directly to the literature that inspired by Siebert *et al.'s* grounding study (1956) assesses the links between distinctive political regimes and the media. More than fifty years of vast but dispersed research proves that constrained notions of normativity linking authoritarianism with media control and democracy with freedom of expression are problematic. Broad distinctions between authoritarianism and democracy do not just hinder crucial divergences within authoritarian rules and within democracies. Raw models for the state-media relation also obscure the influence that a variety of actors, processes, beliefs and legacies from the past impose on this interaction.

Undoubtedly, the labels (Authoritarian, Libertarian, Social Responsibility, developmental, Western) that academic research has used to describe different kinds of relationships between political regimes and media systems were useful here to study the Mexican case and other transitional democracies. But, as seen, these rigid categorisations (named ideal typologies, models or even theories) serve more as descriptive tools than as totalising concepts. Neither Mexican authoritarianism nor the relatively new democratic rule fit perfectly in a single category. This chapter has shown that the assumption of Mexican authoritarianism as a repressive and almighty controlling force over a submissive and powerless commercial media is problematic. This stance not only creates a false image about the actual functioning and goals of mass communication during the authoritarian era, but also hides more complex and interdependent relationships between the authoritarian rule and the media.

Something similar happens in regard to the aspirations set by the Libertarian model of state-media relations in democracies. From this theoretical stance, the Mexican media are expected to be a reliable means of relevant information; to function as guarantors of freedom of speech; to denounce potential abuses from political elites; to give voice to different social and political groups and enhance civic and political participation, to mention some of the stereotypes that media studies usually take for granted but that are simply unrealistic (see for instance: Keane 1991; Scammell and Smetko 2000b; Graber 2003; Gans 2003; Schudson 2003).

Nowadays, Mexican media actually face internal and contextual challenges that restrain their potential to thrive as a vigorous Fourth Estate. The myth is thus not just about the form and functioning of state-media relations during authoritarian rule. The capacity of the change of political regime to transform media into a propeller of democracy also requires further scrutiny. As seen in this chapter, the state-media relationship in Mexico is better described as a mixture of practices, aspirations and overlapping elements of different theoretical models of state-media relations. This approach prevents 'zero-sum game' analyses that overemphasise the control that the state lost and the power that media acquired with the democratic transition. Plus, it encourages a revision of the role (beyond control and repression) that state actors, especially the new governing elites, have played in moulding the structure, functioning and performance of the media in the Mexican democracy.

It is difficult, however, to draw solid conclusions from a single-case study. Nevertheless, the other national cases broadly reviewed in this chapter also point to a cautionary story about the prospects for democracy to take root when the relationship between the state (especially its governing elites) is kept in the shadows. The next chapter of this book introduces an alternative perspective to study the state-media relation. The proposal is to search for an alternative point of entry into the analysis moving the searchlight from normative perspectives to the actual functioning of this relationship.

Notes

1. In the 1988 general election, the PRI won 265 deputies, the lowest number of representatives in the Lower Chamber for the party ever and just above the 251 required seats to reach an absolute majority in that chamber. In that election, the PRI also lost four seats on the Upper Chamber, breaking the monopoly that it historically had had over the Senate.
2. The first electoral victories of an opposition party occurred in 1983 when the PAN won five state capitals: Chihuahua (recovered by the PRI in 1986), Durango, San Luis Potosí, Hermosillo, Guanajuato and a major city, Ciudad Juárez. These defeats were followed by the loss of major cities like Mérida in 1988 and the first defeat at the federal level when the PAN won the state government of Baja California in 1989.
3. This was actually the case of Televisa, nowadays, the biggest broadcaster for the Spanish-speaking market in Latin America.

3 Thinking Institutionally About Politics and the Media

Why and How

> An alternative story emphasizes the role of institutions. The exchange vision of human nature as static and universal and unaffected by politics is replaced by a view of the political actor as flexible, varied, malleable, culture-dependent and socially constructed [. . .] The core notion is that life is organized by sets of shared meanings and practices that come to be taken as given for a long time. Political actors act and organize themselves in accordance with rules and practices which are socially constructed, publicly known, anticipated and accepted.
>
> James March and Johan Olsen, *Institutional Perspectives on Political Institutions* (1996)

This book argues that a narrow notion of normativity that more common than not conceals behind rigid categorisations of media systems, imposes certain risks to the analysis of the state-media relationship. In a context where not only democracies (old and new) are facing numerous challenges, but also the media (old and new platforms) seem to be struggling to adjust equally to new technologies than to consumers' demands, abilities and preferences, alternative (but common) research routes are needed. Furthermore, global trends demand reconsidering the conceptual boundaries and the limitations of the nation state as the representative unit of analysis. In other words, exploring the global or transitional aspects of the interactions between the state and the media goes far beyond granting that different political systems yield different media systems.

As an effort to address some of these challenges, this chapter proposes 'thinking institutionally' (Heclo 2008) about the state-media relationship. That is, instead of purely focusing on ideal typologies or on the kind of relationship politics that the media *should* engage with (as the one proposed by Siebert and his colleagues in *Four Theories of the Press* and strengthened by an ample range of studies that have followed this lead), this perspective argues that the nature and actual the form of the relationships between political regimes and media systems are determined not just by prescriptive duties and norms, but by complex interaction of other institutional factors. The call here is thus not to turn away from normative standards or, more simply, what the state-media relation should be. But it certainly is an appeal to recalibrate the balance between the normative and the descriptive emphases in the study of media systems.

The State-Media Relation: A Supra Institution

It might not be entirely wrong to assume that a key aspect contributing to the poor health of democracy all over the world is the current state of the interaction between politics and the media. Indeed, research on the relationship between politics (politicians, political parties, candidates, government officials) and the media (journalists, media owners, editors) points at the shortcomings of contemporary political communication (Swanson 1992, 1997). More often than not, this literature leads to suspect that neither politicians nor the media are fulfilling the democratic duties imprinted in a normative approach to the state-media relation. While mass media are obsessed with the trivia of endless political campaigning, politicians are prone to hide their flaws and ultimate political goals behind highly crafted political advertising campaigns and media management strategies. From this stance, academic research actually serves as a warning: practically without standing the national context, all over the globe political communication is regularly oversimplified, personalised, trivialised and dramatised as an entertainment show for popular consumption (Entman 1989; Jamieson 1992; Swanson 1992: 397; Patterson 1994).

These recurrent complaints, however, tend to point to the shortcomings between normative ideal types and the actual functioning of the state-media relation. By placing the searchlight on the social processes and the institutions (assuming politics and the media themselves as institutions) that are at the core of political communication, a different picture emerges:

> Politics, government and news media are linked in a complicated relationship and combine to create a kind of *supra-institution*, the political-media complex. Within this complex, particular institutional interests often conflict with each other in the battle of the public's perceptions, but mutual cooperation is required for each institution to achieve its aims [. . .] politicians cannot succeed without access to the media, just as reporters cannot succeed without access to political leaders.
>
> (Swanson 1992: 399, emphasis added)

From this stance, the notion of 'political-media complex' represents a window of opportunity to depart from research grounded on models or ideal types to explain (mainly categorise) the relationship between politics and the media (like *Four Theories of the Press* and its legacy). First, it advances an approach to the relationship between politics and the media that, instead of focusing on the kind of relationship that these two institutions *should* engage with, favours an empirical analysis. What determines the nature and the actual form of the relationship between the state and the media are not just prescriptive principles and duties, but are also an intricate set of institutional factors such as structure, organisational dynamics and history.

Box 3.1 The Political-Media Complex: Advantages of an Institutional Approach to the State-Media Relation

- Provides an alternative approach to accounts that either privilege a story of a complete transformation from authoritarianism to democracy or place emphasis on the 'authoritarian legacies' or 'path dependences' that prevent a new interaction
- Draws the analysis from the great expectations imposed by the democratic model of state-media relations to the actual dilemmas that actors in the political communication sphere face in practice
- Recognises the links and interdependence that tie together the political regime and the media
- Unpacks the interaction between the state and the media into different conceptual and analytical tools

---

This leads to a second key point: the relationship between the institutions of politics and the media themselves as institutions is not assumed as a set of fixed normative preconditions. The value of normative approaches like Siebert *et al.*'s (1956) and subsequent similar theoretical proposals remains an idealised conception of appropriate procedures and desired outcomes. For those in the field, these models set an example and some boundaries to their day-to-day practices. For academics, such theoretical abstractions serve as working hypotheses to assess the actual functioning and consequences of this interaction. An institutional perspective, however, approaches the interaction between politics and the media as a combination of both a 'constantly evolving' interaction between the normative ideal and the particular needs of two set of institutions (political institutions and media institutions) and their respective professionals. The political-media complex request thus a compound analysis of the normativity but also of the structure, functioning and personnel that link together those institutions. It is al also a reminder that this interaction is 'a product of a particular history'

(Swanson 1997: 1266), and in this sense, both the history of each institution and the history of the interaction between politics and the media set the context to understand the actual nature of this relationship.

Third, even when both kinds of institutions have their own history, institutional needs, structure and culture that make them two independent actors, they are also, 'interdependent, and thus, their respective agendas and institutional needs provide incentives for cooperation, as well as conflict' (Swanson 1997: 1266). Admittedly, interdependence between the political regime and the media is not exclusive to Swanson's notion of political-media complex. Other analytical approaches assessing the relationship between politics and the media in general, or politicians and journalists in particular, have also stressed the links that tie together the media and politics (see for instance: Blumler and Gurevitch 1975, 1995; Gunther and Mughan 2000a; Hallin and Mancini 2004a; Ross 2010). Since both institutions (from politics on the one hand, from the media on the other) relay on each other, research on the state-media relation tends to conclude that the media does mirror the social and political structures in which it is embedded (Siebert *et al.* 1956: 1). The political-media complex, however, stresses the interdependence between politics and the media not just as a matter of mutual need of information resources and outlets, or even exclusively as a matter of power. It actually points at 'an unending spiral of manipulation and resistance within a struggle for dominance [. . . that] occurs within the framework of institutions that have been weakened and challenged by a host of changes to which [politicians and the media] constantly struggle to adapt' (Swanson 1997: 1270).

Fourth, the notion of political-media complex warns (as Eisenhower's mention of a 'military-industrial complex' did in the 1960s) of the dangers of this interaction. The relationship between politics and the media influences every aspect of political life: the way in which citizens make sense of their political context and their capacity to influence it; the way in which politicians communicate with citizens; and the way in which mass media present the news about politics to citizens. Research on politics and the media shows that the risks embedded in this process are many: from citizens transformed into armchair consumers of news about politics (Sartori 1987; Entman 1989; Jamieson 1992; Patterson 1994) to 'media-driven republics' (Mazzoleni and Schulz 1999). In this overwhelmingly feared scenario, the presentation of politics as 'show-biz' elevates political campaigns, personality and performance above the substantial issues of political life (Franklin 1994). Plus, this kind of political communication undermines traditional democratic institutions and creates a 'spiral of cynicism' (Cappella and Jamieson 1997) that legitimizes the 'mediatisation of politics' (Blumler and Kavanagh 1999; Mazzoleni and Schulz 1999) and prevents citizens to participate in the political process (Bennett 1988; Zaller 1998).

Last but not least, from this stance citizens' civic engagement in politics is treated as a valuable commodity that shifts the balance of power between politicians and the media (Swanson 1992: 399). Participation, public debate and civic engagement are, however, not necessarily the ultimate goals of this interaction as a normative stand predisposes. Rather, political and media institutions are caught in endless tensions between cooperation and struggle. In this constant battle, the final goal becomes the need to keep the state-media relation afloat, while both sets of institutions relegate citizens (voters or consumers) to mere passive spectators, and citizens themselves seem to passively assume this role.

In a nutshell, this book claims that the notion of a 'political-media complex' represents a useful theoretical alternative to assess this interaction between political regimes and the media. Instead of looking at the state-media relation as a set of ideal types grounded on specific normative guidelines, this approach opens the analysis to diverse institutional aspects of both politics and the media such as organisational structures and procedures, culture, history, power, conflict, interdependence and mutual risks that shape this interaction (Swanson 1997: 1272).

Moving From a Normative to an Institutional Stance: Risks and Implications

Operationalising an institutional analysis of the state-media relationship is, however, a risky enterprise. Institutionalism, as leading researchers stress, is a contested field that 'comes in many flavours' (March and Olsen 2009: 160). More often than not, writes Heclo (2008: 43): 'reviews of the scholarly literature on institutions are an invitation to frustration'. Similarly, Peters (2012: 1) acknowledges that: 'there are a number of alternative conceptions of the approach that may weaken its capacity to serve as an alternative to more individualistic approaches to politics'.

Work on the influence of institutions in the actual functioning of political life nourishes a thriving academic industry. This book, however, evades as much as possible particular debates among or within distinctive neo-institutionalism scholarly traditions.[1] Rather than focusing on a single school of thought, the study of the interaction between politics and the media benefits more from a comprehensive and general institutional approach. The bet is, borrowing Hall's (2010: 220) words, 'that [the] greatest advances will be made by those willing to borrow concepts and formulations from multiple schools of thought'.

However, this is not to say that this approach ignores the crucial divergences between the different disciplines of political science that study institutions from very diverse angles. Nor to disregard that each of these schools of thought bring key insights to the notion of political-media complex (see below). When arguing for an institutional approach, rather than privileging one neo-institutionalism school of thought over the other, this book is more concerned with key institutional factors that are common ground for different academic perspectives. It is also grounded on a notion of democracy that inevitably evokes an ideal approach to mass communication grounded on normative notions such as diversity, accountability, freedom of expression, representation, competition or participation. 'Blended thinking', writes Heclo (2008: 58), 'is not the same thing as sloppy eclecticism. [. . .] It is saying that there is probably more to be gained by combining and exploiting the various schools' insights than by adhering slavishly to their scripts'.

Institutionalism, as the term is used in this book, suggests thus a general approach to the endogenous nature and social construction of institutions that takes into consideration a wider context as well as other characteristics such as organisational structure, agency, performance and institutional change (Olsen 2007: 2). With this in mind, thinking institutionally about the state-media relation implies approaching it as a set (a complex) of interactions in which both the state and the media are themselves institutions. From this stance, the analysis focuses on three core assumptions that, at their root, unify different neo-institutionalism schools of thought. These are: (1) institutions are collections of rules and norms that shape individual behaviour and determine the outcomes of political processes; (2) institutions are structures of resources and meaning that empower or constrain actors' capabilities of action, and; (3) institutions are markers of history, change and stability.[2]

Naturally, there is the possibility of alternative institutional factors that could be considered as similarities between different schools of thought that make neo-institutionalism a unified theoretical perspective.[3] However, the three particular aspects presented in these pages point at both the endogenous and exogenous factors underlined in the notion of political-media complex. 'Of course', writes Swanson (1997: 1272), 'institutions do not act; people act. However, [. . .] people act within institutional contexts, and their actions are inevitably shaped by institutional objectives, organization, culture and history'.

Box 3.2 Institutionalism for the Study of the State-Media Relations

1. Institutions are collections of rules and norms that shape individual behaviour and determine the outcomes of political processes.
2. Institutions are structures of resources and meaning that empower or constrain actors' capabilities of action.
3. Institutions are markers of history, change and stability.

Prescriptive Rules and Appropriate Actions

An analysis of statutory rules and formal norms is certainly a traditional starting point of institutional theory in understanding political phenomena (Eckstein 1979; Hall 1986: 19–23; Peters 2012: Ch. 1). In political science, institutions are commonly, although not exclusively,[4] analysed as the diverse administrative, legal and political formal regulatory frameworks that provide procedural advantages and impediments for individual action (Rhodes 1995; Thoening 2003; Peters 2012). Neo-institutionalists, however, question the usefulness of an approach to rules and norms that render mere descriptions about statutory regulations or prescriptions for formal structures or organisational functioning. Alternative ideas and hypotheses about the role of rules and legal norms in organising political life arise for instance from clarifications about how the formal structures and rules embedded in different forms of government (presidential or parliamentary, for instance) impose distinctive influences on the performance of governmental institutions and also intriguingly shape the way in which individuals behave within these institutions (Hall 1986; Peters 2005: 2). From this perspective, statutory rules and legal norms appear more as 'institutions rather than as instruments' (Brunsson and Olsen 1997: 20).

Broadly speaking, when referring to 'rules', neo-institutionalism theory puts forth a behavioural approach to statutory regulations and formal legal conventions (Olsen 2007: 2). Statutory regulations and other formal rules (for instance, secondary legislations, organisational norms or codes) constitute symbols, scripts and templates for individual behaviour that are beyond rational calculation or self-interests, and that persist over time but are neither stable nor exogenous to individuals' preferences or choice (Swilder 1986; March and Olsen 1989: Ch3; Hall and Taylor 1996: 948). In other words, from a neo-institutional perspective, rulings and formal norms provide codes of meaning that shape individuals' action, facilitate interpretation and reduce ambiguity. In so doing, rules coordinate many simultaneous activities in a way that make individual actions mutually consistent and predictable (North 1981: Ch1).

Different theoretical variations of neo-institutionalism, however, offer diverse explanations about why and how formal rules impose such constraints to individual behaviour. For instance, what Peters (2007: 19) refers to as 'normative neo-institutionalism' puts emphasis on rules and norms as a way to understanding how individual behaviour becomes a ruled-governed 'routine way in which people do what they are supposed to do' (March and Olsen 1989: 21). From this perspective, the relevance of rules in an institutional analysis rests on the 'beliefs, paradigms, codes, cultures, and knowledge that surround, support, elaborate, and contradict those roles and routines' (March and Olsen 1989: 22). Thus, rules are followed because they are seen as natural, rightful, expected and legitimate. In so doing, individuals' actions respond to a 'logic of appropriateness' rather than to a logic of consequence embedded on explanations based on pure rational action (March and Olsen 1989, 1996: 252, 2004). But here 'appropriateness' refers not just to what is right to do according to formal regulations. It also points to a specific culture in which members of an institution are expected to obey and be the guardians of the institution's constitutive principles and standards (March and Olsen 2009: 163).

Alternatively, an approach to institutions from an economist position, which in the literature is often referred as 'rational choice institutionalism', stresses that formal rules are relevant for the analysis of institutions because they represent patterns in which individuals make rational choices. The role of institutions in political life is, therefore, not just restricted to the connection between rules and behaviour. Statutory laws along with other formal norms also influence the way in which individuals define their preferences and select the range of strategies (behaviours) that they will follow to maximise their personal utility (North 1981; Hall and Taylor 1996: 942–946). Rules and norms reduce uncertainty and shape the way in which individuals make decisions in order to maximise the benefits they receive from observing these formal rulings (North 1981; Posner 1993). Therefore, legislations, organisational norms and codes of conduct are both indicators of common acceptable behaviour and predictors of regular outcomes that bring benefits to individuals within and outside a particular institution.

Historical institutionalism, on the other hand, approaches institutions as both formal organisations and informal rules that structure conduct. From this stance, political actors are not purely rational 'maximizers', but rather 'rule-following satisfiers' (Hall and Taylor 1996: 939). Political life is not a mere reflection of individuals looking to maximise self-interests. Individual behaviour is also deeply influenced by experience and 'societally defined rules' (Thelen and Steinmo 1992: 8). Plus, individual strategies and goals are also constrained by an institutional context and history. Past events and previous individual choices also impose certain influence in the course of action at both individual and institutional levels.

Neo-institutional sociologists (sociological institutionalism), in contrast, are more concerned with rules and formal norms as propellers of organisational efficiency and legitimacy. From this stance, regulations and norms become 'socially legitimated rationalized elements' that influence not just the way in which individuals behave, but also how organisations justify their form and functioning within and outside the organisation. In so doing, rules also become resources and capabilities for the survival of the organisations in a constantly changing environment (Meyer and Rowan 1977). Institutions appear, thus, not just as a product of shared rules, norms or common routines and practices, but they also reflect individual actions and culture. Rules and formal norms are also symbols of systems, cognitive scripts and moral templates that provide, as quoted by Hall and Taylor (1996: 947), 'frames of meaning' which guide human actions (original from Campbell 1995).

To recapitulate, for neo-institutionalism theory, the analysis of statutory rules and formal regulations render sound explanations about individual behaviour as a combination of rule-following, indoctrination, experience (history) and choice. However, different schools of thought place the searchlight on distinctive aspects about how and why the analysis of formal rules matters in understanding political phenomena. As Peters (2005: 156) puts it, these differences 'address a classic problem in social analysis—the relatively importance of structure and agency' in explaining political life. Approaches like the normative or the historical neo-institutionalisms regard statutory regulations and formal norms as prime determinants of individual behaviour (see Steinmo 1993: Ch1; March and Olsen 1996). For rational choice and sociological neo-institutionalists, however, individuals are the ones who legitimise and endure these rules by transforming them into particular choices, unwritten codes of conduct or even organisational cultures that persist over time. From this perspective, individuals appear to have more room to shape institutional performance and choices (see for instance: Kreps 1990).

As stated earlier, rather than privileging one school of thought over the other, this book benefits from a more general institutional approach to rules and formal norms. This stance allows an investigation of the formal rulings that shape the relation between political regimes and the media. It also enhances an assessment on how these rules impose (or not) values and norms that might have certain influence on shaping or even changing these formal rulings.

Organisational Dynamic: The Endogenous Nature of Reality

Thinking institutionally about the state-media relation also proposes a deeper analysis of the connection between institutional forms and organisational routines. As Heclo (2008: 62) puts it: 'to study institutions is essentially equivalent to studying formal organizations'. Institutions are meant to mobilise human and material resources by organising these means into effective actions. From this stance, institutions appear not just as mere prescriptive regulatory instruments and exogenous forces. They are also endogenous organisational structures and functions that influence behaviour, construct meaning and shape interests at both organisational and individual levels.

'Institutions', write March and Olsen (1989: 162), 'not only respond to their environments but create those environments at the same time'. From this stance, neo-institutionalism theory suggests a number of ways in which internal organisational forces influence individual preferences and vice versa. For instance, drawing on organisational theory, sociological institutionalists are particularly interested in culturally-specific practices that affect organisational forms and individual behaviour (Hall and Taylor 1996: 946). Rather than taking individual choices within organisations as highly strategic, intentional and predictable (as rational choice institutionalists tend to do), this approach looks at behaviour in cultural terms. This perspective assumes behaviour as tightly bound up with values and norms, but also as shared interpretations of symbols and common moral temples that affect the way in which individuals make choices (Meyer and Rowan 1977; Meyer and Scott 1992: Ch. 1).

Against a 'calculus approach' (Hall and Taylor 1996: 939) whereby individuals seek to maximise personal utility, 'a cultural approach' offers a comprehensive explanation about the attitudes of political actors and common values that influence rational choices. Culture is thus approached not exclusively as individual beliefs and norms, but also as a network of routines, symbols and scripts providing templates for social action (Almond and Verba 1963; Elster 1989). From this stance, the internal processes of institutions and their relationships with other institutions in the same organisational field become key in understanding how individuals internalise their role within organisations like public offices (Peters 2012: 128). The general picture provided by this line of work is one in which, as Powell and DiMaggio (1991: 8) put it: 'while institutions are certainly the result of human activity, they are not necessarily the products of conscious design'. Formal rules give form to organisations, but their functioning and the culture in which they are embedded also determine their shape and the role that individuals play within these organisations.

This is not to say that other neo-institutional approaches, like historical or rational choice institutionalism, deny that organisations or institutions provide structure and behavioural temples for individual or collective action. Nevertheless, the interest of these approaches on organisational structures, skills and learning processes as endogenous institutional forces is primarily as agents of institutionalisation and institutional change. Organisations, writes North (1981: 5), 'are created with purposive intent in consequence of the opportunity set resulting from the existing set of constraints (institutional ones as well as the traditional ones of economic theory) and in the course of attempts to accomplish their objectives are a major agent of institutional change'.

Similarly, from an historical perspective, endogenous formal structures and organised practices play a key role in how organisations function and persist over time. Institutions are embedded in a broader environment in which both endogenous organisational and contextual characteristics influence, for example, how power is distributed within and across different social and political groups. Power and other factors such as leading ideas or past experiences thus become key variables in explaining not just the functioning, but also the origins and persistence of organisations.

History, Change and Continuity

One of the main challenges of thinking institutionally about the state-media relation is that, as institutionalists write (Mahoney and Thelen 2010: 5): 'the idea of persistence of some kind is virtually built into the very definition of an institution. This is true for sociological, rational-choice, and historical-institutional approaches'. From this perspective, institutions are thus not mere reflections of current organisational forces, formal proscriptions, behavioural templates or shared identities. They are also products of past experiences and history. In the end, as March and Olsen (1989: 167–168) puts it: 'institutions embed historical experience into rules, routines, and forms that persist beyond the historical moment and condition'.

Nonetheless, different schools of neo-institutionalism thought offer quite diverse (and complex) explanations about how institutions emerge, endure or change. Rational choice institutionalists for instance, explain the persistence of an institution looking at the benefits it delivers. From this approach, institutions endure partly because they are efficient or cost-effective and partly because individuals make choices according to the information (frequently incomplete) they receive. These choices might not be always optimal and may have unintended consequences that prevent organisations from incremental efficiency. Institutions keep on such a path, writes North (1981: 9), 'because the transaction cost of the political and economic markets of those economies together with the subjective models of the actors do not lead them to move incrementally toward more efficient outcomes'. Institutions do change and new institutions do add to the existing institutional world. However, these changes are seldom discontinuous but rather are incremental and a product of exogenous forces of change. Past choices and imperfect information, for instance, commonly influence the way in which individuals interpret their environment, making existing institutions stable and durable (North 1981: Ch. 1).

Similarly, historical neo-institutionalists put forward the notion of 'path dependence' to explain how policies introduced at one time affect political outcomes at a latter moment (for literature reviews on this concept see: Mahoney 2000; Alexander 2001; Thelen 2004; Pierson 2004). Weir (1992: 192) surmises this process as 'decisions that at one point in time can restrict future possibilities by sending policy off onto particular tracks, along which ideas and interest develop and institutions and strategies adapt'. From this stance, understanding how institutions change requires assessing the direct precedent form or related institutional forms that may affect their current state. A historical approach to institutions accounts for the legacies of past struggles of power, along with particular current environmental contexts (Mahoney and Thelen 2010: 6–7). However, similar operative forces of change rarely generate the same results everywhere (in different countries for instance) mainly because diverse contextual factors, commonly inherited from the past, mediate these forces producing different institutional outcomes (Hall and Taylor 1996: 941).

Sociological institutionalists, in contrast, use concepts such as 'isomorphism' to explain both change and continuity within and among organisations. Broadly speaking, the argument is that organisations face similar constraints (such as contextual, economic or normative) forcing them to resemble other organisations that face similar environmental contexts in a process that push them toward homogenisation (Hawley 1968 as summarised by Powell and DiMaggio 1991: 66). Several factors account for this isomorphism among organisations like norms, learning processes or professionalisation, environmental conditions, market competition, niche measures, economic fitness, other organisations, power, legitimacy and uncertainty, among others. Overall, these factors help to explain, for instance, why inefficient organisations persist over time, how new organisations enter the field or which organisations are predestined to substantive failure. New institutions or institutional change 'borrow' ideas and strategies from the existing world of institutional templates. Why certain institutional templates are chosen over others go beyond considerations of efficiency to incorporate 'an appreciation of the role that collective processes of interpretation and concerns for social legitimacy play in the process' (Hall and Taylor 1996: 953).

This stance, however, tends to lose sight of the contention and clash of power that other neo-institutional approaches have traced in the course of institutional reforms and change. For instance, rational-choice institutionalists argue that processes of institutional creation or change are more about power and competing interests rather than about collective frames of meaning, scripts and symbols (see for instance: Knight 1992: Ch1; Moe 2005). Alternatively, historical institutionalists look at particular moments or events where agents were able to modify past practices and trajectories (Rokkan and Lipset 1967: 37; Katznelson 2003; Capoccia and Kelemen 2007). What rests from these debates is the duality of continuity and change. That is, even when the notion of an institution rest on a common understanding of persistence, endurance and continuity, institutions do change. But this change cannot be explained without looking at the continuities from past practices or forms.

The Political-Media Complex: An Alternative Analytical Framework

An institutional approach to the state-media relation is useful to integrate separate lines of research into a comprehensive conceptual framework to study the state-media relation. Table 3.1 below shows how the institutional factors identified in the previous section of this chapter are operationalised to assess the interaction between distinctive political regimes and media systems. As discussed these are: (1) the rules institutions enforce to give order; (2) the organisational dynamic institutions impose over individuals' roles, and (3) the patterns and tendencies that institutions take from but also use to shape historical rules and practices.

Thinking institutionally about rules, as proposed in this book, implies an approach to both formal rules and to what neo-institutionalists call 'appropriate behaviour'. Therefore, as shown in Table 3.1, prescriptive rules are investigated through constitutional rights and duties, specific statutory legislation, particular policies, organisational norms, internal rules of procedures or codes of conduct. This normative perspective is complemented with the analysis of informal templates for individual behaviour such as culture, common understandings or knowledge. Admittedly, 'appropriateness' as described by neo-institutionalists is an abstraction and as such, it is unfeasible to precisely measure it with empirical data. Nevertheless, descriptions about the orientations and beliefs of key actors in communicating politics serve to confront what is written in formal rules with what it is actually happening in the field.

Indeed, the study of the state-media relation in old and new democracies has rendered key insights about the role that both aspects (prescriptive regulatory frameworks and 'appropriateness') play in this interaction. Broadly speaking, the scope and form of statutory regulation define the form and functioning of distinctive media systems around the world (Nieminen 2016; Lunt and Livingstone 2011; Feintuck and Varney 2006). Public service broadcast systems (more relevant in Europe) impose particular normative assumptions and rationales for both the state as a regulatory agent and the media as an entertainment industry. These systems also approach the media as guarantors of public accountability and propellers of citizens' engagement and participatory debate. A healthy media system is one where the state supports the media in fulfilling these tasks. Statutory regulation is then seen as both necessary and desirable to sustain the conditions for a vibrant Fourth Estate to thrive. Media regulation helps to shield media

Table 3.1 Thinking Institutionally About the State-Media Relation in New Democracies: An Alternative Conceptual Framework

Institutional Factors	Components	Analytical tools	
Rules	Prescriptive Rules		Constitutional rulings
			Particular legislation
			Organisational norms, internal rulings or particular codes of conduct
	Appropriate actions		Beliefs, paradigms, codes
			Culture and knowledge
Organisational dynamic	Organisational charts	Human Resources	Recruitment processes
			Professional profiles: background and skills
			Training
		Financial Resources	Budget
			Contracts
			Disclosure mechanisms
	Practices and day-to-day routines	Strategic Communication	Communication objectives: planning and coordination
		Political logic	Information gathering: evaluation processes of media and political environments
		Media logic	Information dissemination: communication channels
	Measures of public response and evaluation mechanisms		Role of the public in the design and functioning of communication strategies
			Feedback and public opinion surveys
Patterns of change and continuity	The professionalisation of political communication		Alternative homogenisation patterns: modernisation, Americanisation, globalisation
			Interrelated changes in politics, the news media and in communicating politics
			Authoritarian legacies, path dependences and continuities

markets from concentration, and at the time it guarantees the access of all to a broad diversity of (preferably high-quality) media contents. Regulation becomes then a useful measure to ensure that citizens are protected from being treated as mere consumers of media products (see for instance: Lunt and Livingstone 2011: Ch. 1).

In contrast, commercial media systems (more relevant in the U.S. and in Latin America, for instance) assume the market of being capable to regulate the media. In general terms, mass communication (media contents or platforms) is seen as a commodity available only to those willing to pay for it. Thus, state regulation can be limited to mere technical matters such as wavelength scarcity or network architecture. The forces of the market (open competition, diversity of platforms or changing preferences on the demand of services) serve as self-regulatory measures. By itself, the market is able to face other challenges such as the ones imposed by developments in the industry, changes in the characteristics of audiences (age or preferences, for instance), the emergence of new media platforms and new communication technologies.

In addition, diverse cultural and behavioural aspects broaden these distinctive conceptions about media regulation (Hallin and Mancini 2004a: 55–56). For instance, the degree to which citizens, business and other actors are willing to follow formal rules and serve the public good, instead of evading regulations in the pursuit of self-interest is a key determinant of the media's functioning (Hallin and Mancini 2004a: 56). In other words, regulation (whether it is by the state or by the market) shapes the way in which the media functions not only by proscribing certain duties and rights, but also by imposing a set of beliefs, unwritten norms and patterns of behaviour to the political-media complex.

This book argues that analyses on media regulation improve when taking into consideration both, the formal and written statutory rulings or proscriptions, as well as the influence of diverse cultural and behavioural aspects. This approach is particularly relevant on the study of transitional democracies. More common than not, in these countries statutory regulation (or the lack of it) perpetuates mechanisms of government manipulation and constrains the Fourth Estate to market demands and economic designs that favour the development of powerful entertainment industries (see for instance: Waisbord 2000; de Smaele 1999; Wasserman and de Beer 2006; Lugo-Ocando 2008).

For instance, in Latin America, both the political and commercial logics are present and closely linked to media regulation. This interdependence sets both certain needs for and limits to media regulation. For the media to thrive as a democratic political institution, a strong presence of the state has been necessary to regulate market concentration or to protect journalists from threats and pressures emerging from both political actors and media moguls (Waisbord 2007, 2010). On the other hand, antiquated and hostile legislations (such as criminal defamation laws; the lack of effective access to government information laws or weak legal measures to protect journalists' confidential sources) inhibit media's capacity to enhance public scrutiny, strengthen political accountability and promote assertive reporting (Lawson and Hughes 2005a; Matos 2008; McPherson 2012). Plus, 'political clientelism' still tends to define the relationship between new democracies and the media (Hallin and Papathanassopoulos 2002). This points to the persistence of past practices and mindsets about the rule of law and the political use of the media. 'A culture in which evasion of the law is relatively common', write Hallin and Papathanassopoulos (2002: 187), 'means that opportunities for particularistic pressures also are common: governments can exercise pressure by enforcing the law selectively, and news media can do so by threatening selectively to expose wrongdoing'.

Thinking institutionally about the state-media relation, as shown in Table 2.1 (above), proposes then to complement the analysis on the rules that govern the state-media relation (media regulation) with the examination of common understandings and beliefs about the rule of law (about compliance or enforcement) that more common than not, impose additional challenges and limitations to regulatory processes.

For its part, the organisational dynamic of the state-media relation is studied through three aspects: (1) organisational charts; (2) practices and day-to-day routines; (3) strategies to measure public responses. This selection might seem arbitrary to experts. Especially when, as shown in Table 3.1, each of these dimensions includes concepts that have individually generated ample academic debate. Nevertheless, according to the literature on the structure and functioning of the media (newsrooms mainly), political campaigning and government communication offices, these components aim at a better understanding on how internal dynamics of the media or politics shape the way in which these entities work and interact with other actors on daily bases. The purpose of putting all these aspects together under the umbrella of 'organisational dynamic' responds to the need, as proposed in the political-media complex (Swanson 1992, 1997), of approaching the relation between politics and the media in terms of interdependence and coevolution (Hallin and Mancini 2004a: 47), rather than as autonomous forces.

For instance, as seen in Table 3.1, organisational charts, the first component to study the organisational dynamic of the political-media complex, proposes a closer look at the communication workforce (professional profiles and background, recruitment strategies and training programs), as well as at the budget allocated to the state-media relation. This, naturally, might seem a titanic analytical effort since the resources invested in this interaction are many: from journalists or bureaucrats strictly assigned to all sorts of interactions between the media and the political process (public servants, candidates, congresspersons, etc,) to multimillion political advertising contracts that more common than not, are difficult to trace let alone to audit. The goal of taking a closer look to organisational charts, however, is to have a better understanding of the organisational structure(s),—especially personnel and budget—in which the state-media relation is embedded.

In this task, admittedly, highly crafted political communication and information management strategies should not be a surprise. The mere fact that modern democracies invest significant human and financial resources in information services and press-offices is in line with a long and well-known practice of professional and crafted political communication (see for example: Katz and Lazarsfeld 1955; Rubin 1958; Rogers 1983; Bennett 1988; Johnson-Cartee and Copeland 2004; Scammell 2014). What worries political communication scholars and practitioners, however, is the sudden growth and wide-scale adoption of these practices. Politicians and the media retain the goal to communicate politics to citizens, but the practices regularly used nowadays aim at managing, tailoring and selectively disseminating public information.

Hence, researchers' suspicions are about increasing budgets and personnel involved in the state-media relation, but also about its consequences. Widely spread among scholars is the notion that designing political or government communication campaigns as if politicians were soap, or reporting them as if they were in a horse race is increasingly becoming an empty (but common) practice (Gitlin 1991). The risks of 'packaging politics' (Franklin 1994) are not just about bringing to the public sector advertising and marketing techniques widely used in the private sector. 'Infotainment' (Blumler 1992; Brants 1998; Delli Carpini and Williams 2001) highlights the drama about a political life in which personality, strategy and performance receive more attention than substantive issues such as policy-making, representation or participation. Media restrict other actors' access to mass communication, selectively privileging certain kinds of information and treating politics as show business (see for example: Bennett and Entman 2001; Price *et al.* 2002; Graber 2003; Habermas 2006; Voltmer 2006; Gaber 2007). Reducing politics to sound bites (Hallin 1992) increases citizens' cynicism about politics: its participants, processes and key functions in society (Cappella and Jamieson 1997).

Having a closer look at the organisational charts that put the state-media relation at work pursues a critical analysis of what resources—who (personnel), as well as how (budgets)—the media and politicians are deploying when interacting to each other. As explained, the final goal of this approach is to move the searchlight from a normative stance that explains *why* political regimes and media systems are close related, to an institutional approach that allows a closer look of *how* this relation actually functions.

As shown in Table 3.1 (above), two additional aspects complement this approach to the organisational dynamic of the state-media relation. An analysis of the practices and day-to-day routines of the state-media relation recognises that as professions, political journalism and political communication are in indelibly marked by the norms and the course of both politics and the media (see: Cook 1998; Sparrow 1999; Schudson 2002; Davis 2009). For instance, analyses on the relationship between journalists and their sources picture intimate and complex interactions of power, control and most of all interdependent interests and routines between politicians and newsrooms. Rather than a strong and unrestricted control of the state over the media, the picture emerging from these studies is one that resembles more a 'bargaining interplay' (Sigal 1973: 5), 'exchange of information for publicity' (Tunstall 1970: 44), 'negotiated control over the signs and means' (Ericson *et al.* 1989: 376) or even a 'symbiotic relationship' (Mazzoleni and Schulz 1999: 252) or 'danse macabre' (Ross 2010) between journalists and politicians.

In general, these studies serve as a reminder of the potential power (cultural, political or economic) that each entity has to control the state-media relation. Politicians may generally appear as almighty forces capable of influencing or even setting the news agenda (see for instance: Schiller 1973; Murdock and Golding 1977; McAnany *et al.* 1981). Powerful sources appear as the only ones capable of offering 'information subsidies' (Gandy 1982: 8), that is, privileged, manageable or prompt information that reduces the costs embedded in news coverage. Journalists tend to rely on these information subsidies to report the news about politics in what critics have denounced as a 'structured set of preferences by the media to the opinions of the powerful' (Hall *et al.* 1978: 58).

From this stance, news media become the voice of 'primary definers' who enjoy special status and granted access to the public debate. Government communicators actually benefit from the strategic advantages of primary definition by setting the terms of the debate, commanding the discourse, and becoming 'the dominant and consensual connotations' on the public debate (Hall *et al.* 1978: 61). By granting government officials routine access to media coverage, mainstream news media generally appear as mere followers of the 'sphere consensus' (Hallin 1986) that drives the decision-making processes. Journalists might 'calibrate' (Bennett *et al.* 2005: 49) their news coverage by including alternative sources of information. But these voices are brought into the public debate 'according to the range of views expressed in mainstream government debate about the topic' (Bennett 1990: 106). Alternative sources thus face great challenges on accessing media coverage that come from both the power that official sources have to control the news agenda and the practices that journalists follow in news coverage.

For others, however, the interaction between media and politicians appears more as an 'instrumental-utilitarian calculus' (Schlesinger 1990: 79), than as a fixed condition of guaranteed access to positive news coverage for official sources. That is, a closer look to the organisational structure and functioning of the newsrooms shows that the privileged access of official sources to news coverage is more as an ascertainable outcome of day-to-day practices and routines rather than as an a priori effect of power and control. For instance, as alternative sources offer additional valuable information to journalists, official sources gradually lose their granted access to the news agenda. Other sources acquire relevance as they offer additional information, have certain influence on the news agenda or are simply close (geographically or socially) to journalists (Gans 1980: 117). Newsrooms are in fact willing to cover non-official sources mainly because they offer key additional information or expert knowledge; mobilise relatively large groups and audiences; are strategically located, or; prove to have efficient news management skills (see for instance: Goldenberg 1975). In so doing, journalists partially lose their 'secondary role in reproducing the definitions of those who have privileged access' (Hall *et al.* 1978: 59) and become primary definers (Sigal 1986). Assuming guaranteed access to ever powerful and monolithic official sources actually obscures the information flows, contention for media access and the strategic communication practices put forward by non-dominant sources (Schlesinger and Tumber 1994).

In sum, institutional analyses on the structure and functioning of the media have rendered key insights on the routines, values and beliefs of journalists and their newsrooms especially when approaching official sources. 'The central point is that the concept of institutions', writes Kaplan (2006: 174), 'introduces culture and power into the analysis of journalism, overcoming merely technical, naturalistic understandings'. That is, the day-to-day routine of the news media as well as journalists' stance (professional background, ideas and predilections) influence the way in which the media approach their sources and structure news coverage. From this stance, sources' capacity of definition (primary or secondary) appears less as an exclusive prerogative for dominant sources, and more as a handy opportunity for journalists to organise and present the news. In fact, news coverage is turned into proactive journalism through agenda setting (Shaw and McCombs 1977), framing (Gamson 1989) and the inclusion of alternative voices in the public debate (Harrison 1985; Schudson 2002).

For their part, studies on political and government communication show how politicians are also prone to carefully plan and perform their relation with the media through 'strategic communication processes [. . .] in which messages are shaped, tested, evaluated, and revisited until they encourage the desired effect' (Pfetsch 2008: 73; Canel and Sanders 2010). Research identifies two broad types of strategic political communication (Pfetsch 2008). The 'political-logic' or 'party-centred' communication strategy aims to mobilise political support and legitimise public decisions or policies through political communication. The main goal of political communication becomes then to retain political power through official information and public trust. In this process, mass media are 'the means, but not the ends of the action' (Pfetsch 2008: 73). Political discourse and communication techniques are tailored to gain presence or control over potential electoral competition. Government messages, for instance, are aimed to attract popular support while the media's involvement in the process is restricted to their role as broadcasters.

By contrast, the 'media logic' or 'media-centred' news management is concerned with adapting political messages, communication techniques and political actors' image (whether bureaucrats, political parties, politicians or candidates running for office) to media formats, news values and commercial patterns. Media become both the means and the targets of government communication. Mass news media are the main channels of communication to keep citizens informed about public policies and political objectives. Media, moreover, are regarded as key tools in the struggle for political power by attracting audiences, framing the political debate and creating or mobilising popular consent. Political communication, in consequence, gradually moves away from traditional formats such as the press release or the press conference to more strategic, professionalised and technologically-mediated practices that aim at controlling the flow of news. This strategic approach to political communication greatly influences the day-to-day practices and routines that government communicators use to relate with the media and communicate to citizens (Mazzoleni 1987; Mazzoleni and Schulz 1999).

Going back to Table 3.1, an additional dimension of the organisational dynamic explores the use of public response measures and of evaluation mechanisms that assess the impact of these highly crafted process of communication between politicians and the media. Including these analytical tools into the political-media complex recognises evidence on the use of public opinion surveys and evaluation processes as common, yet dangerous tools in communicating politics (see for instance: Scammell 1995; Kurtz 1998; Davis 2002; Strömbäck 2011). The proposal here is to have a closer look of the role that the general public is actually playing in the design and functioning of political communication. Fear among researchers point at strategic communication processes that are tailored according to politicians' or media's needs and processes, while the needs of the general public (information, participation, diversity of voices, debate, etc.) are simply left behind.

Last but not least, as discussed in the previous section of this chapter, the third institutional factor proposed in the political-media complex is addressed throughout patterns of change and continuity. This approach denotes an analysis of diverse trends that give rise to a combination of disruptive change coupled with continuities from the past. Drawing on the notion of 'professionalisation' that encompasses these transformations, the analysis focuses on how particular trends of change coupled with national contexts and the persistence of past practices shape the state-media relation. Furthermore, this approach allows tracing new developments in communication (technological such as the internet, or socio-economic and political globalisation trends) that imposes key conceptual limits to the nation-state as the main unit of analysis for the interaction between politics and the media (Canel and Voltmer 2014: 3).

Indeed, by looking at historical trends and the patterns of change and continuity, political communication research has aimed at explaining striking similarities all over the world. For instance, as a working hypothesis, the concept of 'Americanisation' summarises different trends of change that seem to originate or emanate from the U.S. and are then followed by other countries. Whereas scholars keep struggling with the idea of using the U.S. as an archetype to analyse other media or political systems, they keep referring to 'Americanisation' as an umbrella concept that puts together a broad spectrum of transformations in political communication that occur globally, and apparently regardless of distinctive national political regimes or media systems (Blumler and Gurevitch 1977/1955; Butler and Ranney 1992; Scammell 1995; Kaid and Holtz-Bacha 1995; Swanson and Mancini 1996). Critics to this approach stress that comparative research does point at crucial differences among countries that force the reconsideration of the idea of a final, superior stage towards which all processes of political communication are targeting (see for instance: Negrine and Papathanassopoulos 1996; Scammell 1997; Lilleker and Negrine 2002; Swanson 2004).

Alternatively, the concept of 'homogenisation' also addresses common trends in political communication that occur simultaneously, but have diverse consequences or scope across nations. What at first glance appears as similar political communication practices that follow the American lead or the same technological patterns (Tunstall 1977; Boyd-Barrett *et al.* 1977; Tomlinson 1991), under the scrutiny of comparative research, some useful explanations arise about the diversity of practices and trends of change that are shaped by each national context. From this perspective, an increasingly homogeneous global communication system may resemble structures and routines initially tested in the U.S. Nevertheless, it also recognises, for instance, that diverse countries adapt American political communication practices to their own economic and political processes, often modifying them in significant ways (Hallin and Mancini 2004b: 27).

In sum, current research on political communication and media systems around the world points towards convergence and homogenisation patterns of change in the political-media complex. To better understand these global trends, academics have assessed diverse causes that range from new political and social conditions to the reproduction of (American) political communication models apparently without standing national particularities. It remains difficult however, to predict how far this process of convergence may go, especially when looking at transitional or new democracies where strong authoritarian legacies and path dependencies combined with broad processes of social and political change impose great influence on the state-media relation. Plus, findings on homogenisation patterns of political communication arise from a well-known battery of Western case studies. But these patterns set questions about the conceptual utility of the nation-state as a unit of analysis, especially in a context where the differences between nationally distinctive political regimes diminish, but when endogenous political and social factors are most likely the motors of these changes.

Conclusions

This chapter draws on the notion of political-media complex to introduce an alternative analytical framework to study the state-media relation. 'Thinking institutionally' about the relationship between political regimes and media systems contests broad assumptions about this interaction merely mirroring fixed normative prescriptions or misguided individual choices. If the goal is to sort out the shortcomings of the interaction between politics and the media, it is necessary to understand the institutional forces that better explain its current flaws and potential dangers (Swanson 1992, 1997). Directing the searchlight to institutional factors renders additional evidence on how, and most intriguing why, both media and politicians in new and old democracies are (apparently) predestined to unfulfilling their duties in communicating politics proscribed by the liberal-democratic paradigm. From this standpoint, the following chapter puts the political-media complex at work. It seeks to move the study of the interaction between political regimes and media systems by understanding first, *why* transitional democracies divert so greatly from the Liberal or Social Responsibility ideal types ('theories') and second, *how* this interaction actually *is* instead of what it *should be*.

Notes

1 For reviews about divergences and similarities among different schools of thought see for instance: Hall and Taylor (1996); Kato (1996); Reich (2000); Pierre *et al.* (2008); and Peters (2012).

2 In their early calls for a reappraisal of institutions in political science, March and Olsen (1989: 160) make the clearest description in this respect: 'as a preface of political institutions', these authors stress 'we have identified three broad clusters of ideas. The first emphasises the way in which political life is ordered by rules and organizational forms that transcend individuals and buffer or transform social forces. The second emphasises the endogenous nature of reality, interests and roles, and so a constructive vision of political actors, meanings and preferences. The third emphasizes the history-dependent intertwining of stability and change'. For similar analyses on the fundamental analytic points that bring together distinctive neo-institutionalism perspectives see: Kato (1996) and Pierre *et al.* (2008); and Peters (2012: Ch10).

3 For instance, Peters (2012, 2005) identifies three alternative common features that at their root unify the distinctive proponents of institutional theory: (1) the emphasis that the different approaches place on institutional factors rather than on individual aspects of social analysis; (2) the attention put on the role that institutional structure plays in determining individual behaviour, and (3) the role that institutions play in reducing uncertainty and in creating greater regularities in human behaviour. In contrast, for Hall and Taylor (1996: 937) any institutional analysis seeks a better understanding of: (1) the interaction between structure and individual behaviour, and (2) the processes whereby institutions change. This book builds upon these fundamental points of similarity for institutional analyses rather than on the differences that prevent an approach to neo-institutionalism theory as a unified body of thought.

4 Rhodes (2009), in contrast, distinguishes four examples of different traditions in the study of political institutions. These are: (1) the formal-legal approach that focuses on the study of public laws as shapers of governmental organisations; (2) an approach to the influence that the ideas about public authority impose over the relations between citizens and government; (3) the modernist-empiricism tradition that has grounded current neo-instutionalists approaches to politics, and (4) a socialist perspective that points to class struggle, social engineering and discourse as practices and meanings that also shape social actors' beliefs and performance. Peters (2005: Ch. 1 and 10), however, stresses that there are more than a dozen schools of thought dealing with public institutions. More often than not, these disciplines diverge from common definitions about what an institution is, about how institutions are created, how they change or how they shape individual behaviour.

4 The Political-Media Complex at Work

A New Perspective on the Study of Transitional Democracies

> In practice, however, things are seldom as clear-cut. Problems associated with inherited authoritarian institutions of the formal kind are, in fact, often created and/or compounded by authoritarian cultural or traditional actors, forces, and patterns in society [. . .] The persistence of authoritarian legacies in postauthoritarian democracies may be explained in terms of a combination of socially, culturally and institutionally inducted set of attitudes, perceptions, motivations, and constraints —that is, from traditions or institutions of the past as well as from present political struggles within formally democratic arrangements.
>
> Katherine Hite and Paola Cesarini, *Authoritarian Legacies and Democracy in Latin America and Southern Europe* (2004)

If the time has come to rise above the limitations that rigid typologies bound to an ideal model of liberal democracy imprint over the study of the state-media relation especially in transitional democracies, sharper analytical tools are needed. The change of political regime imposed great expectations that either politicians nor the media are able to fulfil. More common than not, academic research centres the analysis on (and inevitably ends up condemning) both set of actors' failures rather than on politics and the media as institutions. The former stance, however, might have prevented a better understanding of the actual dilemmas that the interaction between these relatively new political regimes and the media faces when transiting from authoritarianism to democracy. The latter, it is here argued, represents an opportunity to move the study of media systems beyond raw categorisations of ideal types that induce constrained notions of normativity.

This chapter uses thus the political-media complex advanced in this book to explore a different research agenda. It addresses the question of how the process of democratisation changed the interaction between the state and the media. But rather than using fixed categorisations grounded on pure normative approaches to conclude that transitional democracies inevitably do not fit, that more media systems categories are thus needed, the following pages look closely at how the complexity of past norms, old practices, new regulatory frameworks, organisational dynamics and a constant dialectic between change and continuity help explain the shortcomings academic research has already uncovered.

Thinking Institutionally About Transitional Democracies: Key Research Questions

How did the process of democratisation change the state-media relation in transitional democracies? There are indeed two dominant but seemingly contradictory narratives to answer this question. On the one hand, there is the story of a state-media relation transformed with the (partial) collapse of authoritarian rules and the rise of democratic regimes all over the world. From this perspective, change from authoritarianism to democracy seems to result in a fundamental new order (Gunther and Mughan 2000b; Price *et al.* 2002; Voltmer 2006). According to the liberal democratic paradigm, the political regime is not the only one expected to promote and protect a free, diverse and independent media. The media themselves also acquire an active and positive role in the political process (McQuail 1992; Christians *et al.* 2009; Curran 2011).

On the other hand, some literature on democratisation draws on concepts such as 'authoritarian legacies' that holds secure to the assumption that past structural conditions and behavioural patterns influence (mostly inhibiting) a more democratic relationship between the state and the media (see for instance: Bermeo 1992; O'Donnell 1996; Hite and Cesarini 2004; Pion-Berlin 2005). This stance is commonly grounded on the assumption that democratisation does not occur on a blank slate. Inherited cultural, social and political traits shape the way in which transitional democracies deal with both the challenges and the opportunities embedded in the change of political regime.

Similarly, the concept of 'path dependence' becomes useful for establishing a link between past experiences and present choices in state-media relations (see for instance: Roudakova 2008; Canel and Sanders 2012; Voltmer 2012; Gross and Jakubowicz 2013). Diverse actors such as policymakers, journalists or media owners tend to support old structures and reproduce traditional patterns of behaviour not just because the political transition involves uncertainty and imposes high costs at least in the immediate and short terms. Authoritarian traits are also self-perpetuating because politicians and media representatives regard certain practices and structures as the usual and the normal way of doing things. To put simply, 'old habits die hard', and from this angle, the state-media relation in new democracies looks very much like it did during the authoritarian era despite several changes in the political context and in the actors or the procedures involved (see for instance: Gross 2002: Ch. 1; Ogundimu 2002; Lugo-Ocando 2008; Voltmer 2013a: Ch. 5; Vaca 2015). The question arises as to how these two contrasting stories of the state-media relation can be reconciled. The answer to this puzzle might come straight away: the state-media relation in transitional democracies lies somewhere between the two poles of change and continuity. That is, from authoritarianism to democracy, the relationship between the state and the media does not change radically; 'path departures' do not occur unexpectedly and significant transformations (if any) are the product of gradual and small changes that take a long time to crystallise. From this angle, the task of the analyst appears to be quite straightforward: to assess if the new political elites either promote or undermine media freedom.

Nevertheless, more common than not, researchers on state-media relations in transitional democracies face great challenges to unpack the notions of state control and media freedom (Waisbord 2013). For instance, certain hypotheses may immediately come to mind regarding the ultimate power that post-authoritarian governing elites may have to control the interaction with the media through ownership, funding, licensing, regulation or even access to public information. However, the connection between state power and media control turns out to be quite problematic. It might be the case that transitional democracies lack the resources that authoritarian rule used to have (secrecy, manipulation, human and financial means) making the imposition of traditional controls and high levels of coercion against the media simply unfeasible. In this context, other (perhaps subtler and less evident) mechanisms of media control become handy such as media management or public advertising (see for instance: Pfetsch and Voltmer 2012; Waisbord 2012; Bajomi-Lázár 2013).

Or it could be that the incapacity of the state to enforce regulations or to protect the media from other threats (such as market concentration or violence against journalists) turns out to be as dangerous and harmful in the light of democratic aspirations for the media as statutory and perverse mechanisms of media control like repression, or censorship (Waisbord 2000; Morris and Waisbord 2001). In addition, diverse conditions within and outside the media may turn them into actors with their own institutionalised sources of power and control (Patterson 2000; Scammell and Semetko 2000b; Herman and Chomsky 2002; Lloyd 2004). This possibility suggests the need to reconceptualise the role (beyond control and repression) of the state and especially of the new governing elites in moulding the structure, functioning and performance of the media in transitional democracies.

Change in the way governing elites relate with the media in these relatively new democracies is also understandably approached with a sense of great disappointment (see for instance: Hydén *et al.* 2002; Voltmer 2006, 2013a; Lugo-Ocando 2008; Gross and Jakubowicz 2013). Research has shown that these new political regimes have frequently failed on setting the rules and the conditions to transform this interaction. The (small) changes found (in the political rule or in the media) have also been shown to be slower than anticipated, uncertain and unsatisfying, especially when matched with the great expectations created by the political transition to democracy. However, it may be for instance that the new governing elites have failed to enhance a media system that supports the development of democracy because they lack the resources (political or financial) to do so; they may actually pursue an instrumental and controlling purpose over the media, or; the actual functioning of this interaction may be a by-product or even an unanticipated result of other conditions associated with the political transition (such as increasing political competition and divergence among different actors). In any case, such explanations (or alternative ones) deserve thoughtful interrogation.

In addition, scholars have struggled to come to terms with empirical evidence pointing at the presence of both changes and continuities in the state-media relation in new democracies. Transformation (change) is commonly associated with disruptive events leading to changes in institutions and practices, while permanence is generally pictured as a symptom of the 'deadweight of the authoritarian past' over the present. Plus, these legacies are commonly seen as determinants for both the quality and the sustainability of a democratic future (see for instance: Gross 2002: Ch1; Ogundimu 2002; Lugo-Ocando 2008; Voltmer 2013a: Ch5). It becomes thus very difficult to assess if the relationship between the state and the media is actually moving forward or backwards in the continuum from authoritarianism to democracy. A failure (from the state or the media) to achieve the expectations imposed by the democratic transition does not necessarily mean that the state-media relation does not change. Nor does the persistence of certain norms and practices imply that there is nothing new emerging between authoritarianism and democracy.

From this stance, key questions remain about the state-media relation in transitional democracies: does the authoritarian past instil a fear of change on balance or does it foster a greater resolve to transform this interaction among political elites? To what extent does the state-media relation follow the flow of inertial institutionalised authoritarian forces that are beyond the control of individuals, or is there evidence of individual agency which also fosters democratic change in the context of political communication?

As an alternative conceptual framework, the political-media complex proposes an investigation of the interaction between the state and the media in transitional democracies which highlights how—and the extent to which—developments lie somewhere between the two poles of change and continuity; between being a product of inertia and innovation; between macro institutional structures or specific process and human agency and micro-decisions. That is, rather than pointing at current afflictions of contemporary political communication by stipulating that it simply 'falls short from the liberal democratic ideal' or 'reflect(s) only loopholes and bad choices made by misguided or unprincipled individuals', the analysis begins with 'the institutional grounding of objectionable practices' (Swanson 1992: 399).

Table 4.1 (below) unpacks these institutional changes into the specific aspects under investigation. The main goal is to scrutinise how the process of democratisation has changed (or perhaps not) the interaction between the state and the media. As seen, some authoritarian traits might remain. But the political-media complex aims at identifying both the causes and consequences of these endurances. In the process, the analysis looks at formal and informal mechanisms that set the parameters for this interaction such as statutory regulation, organisational structures or patterns of change that are common around the world, but that impose particular challenges to these relatively new political regimes.

Table 4.1 The Political-Media Complex: Main Research Questions

1. Central research question:

How did the process of democratisation change
the state-media relation in transitional democracies?

2. Complementary research questions:

How did the new governing cadres and the media manage their relation?
Which formal and informal institutional norms, rules and practices influenced the way these two set of actors interact?

3. Conceptual framework

What is the state of media regulation in these new democracies?	Rules
How do these formal rules and norms impose (or not) certain limits to the state-media relation?	
Do these statutory regulations and norms, as neo-institutionalism theory suggests, trigger an appropriate behaviour for governing elites?	
If so, what, constitutes this 'logic of appropriateness'?	
What is the organisational structure of the state-media relation?	Organisational
How does it function on a day-to-day basis?	Dynamic
Does political communication in these new democracies show signs of the professionalisation trends that research has traced around the world?	Patterns of Change
How does the development of this process shape the state-media relation in these countries?	

In short, grounded on the indication that overly normative conceptions of the state-media relation in new democracies do not seem to address the dilemmas that actors in the political communication sphere face in practice, the political-media complex provide an alternative point of entry to research on this interaction. It allows an examination of the characteristics which give rise to change and those which induce stasis. After all, the way in which continuity and stasis interact and give rise to novel institutional norms and practices particularly in the contexts of emerging democracies remains an underdeveloped area of studies.

The rest of the chapter draws on previous research on transitional democracies in Latin America, Europe and Africa to put the political-media complex at work. While it is certainly difficult to generalise from the range of dissimilar experiences that these relatively new democracies present, the goal in the following pages is twofold: to test the political-media complex, and to pave the road for identifying common patterns that serve to characterise the interaction between political regimes and the media in new democracies. The next sections of the chapter examine thus how the state-media relation in these countries has (or not) developed new regulations, organisational dynamics and political communication strategies. What follows also looks at how the new governing elites and the media have responded to both persistence from the authoritarian past and innovation trends (presumably) imposed by the process of democratisation.

Rules: What For?

Arguing for an analysis of media regulation in a context of a(n apparently) deregulation deluge around the world (especially in Europe) seems puzzling (Braman 2004). One the one hand, according to the liberal democratic paradigm, market liberalisation allows the media to thrive as commercial enterprises which are (finally) free from the shadows of the state. The end of public monopolies and highly concentrated private ownership; as well as an open and competitive access to the industry enables an environment for a truly independent (from the state yet not from the market) media. From this stance, one key indicator of a healthy relationship between the state and the media in transitional democracies could be the form and strength of the media as a business regulated only by the laws of the market.

On the other hand, however, in the name of the 'public good' some limits to (the potentially overwhelming) commercial interests and power of the media are ultimately necessary. In the end, that was the purpose behind Peterson's (1956) use of the notion of 'Social Responsibility' as a key 'theory' of the press. Nevertheless, the goal of an effective media's self-regulation keeps being a recurrent idyllic possibility still beyond reach (Van Cuilenburg and Slaa 1993; Puppis 2010; Van Cuilenburg and McQuail 2010). From this stance, the indicators of a constructive relation between the state and the media in terms of regulation become a full range of statutory legal frameworks to ensure diversity, openness and freedom. State intervention through formal and informal mechanisms aim to organise media's structure, performance and even contents to ensure that citizens (or consumers) get what they need (or want) from the media: be it information, public debate, participation or entertainment (Lunt and Livingstone 2011). More common than not, however, media regulation incorporates a broad range of contradictory statutory regulations (for consumers and for citizens) norms (for the state, the industry, the medium), and informal practices that coexist but are almost impossible to settle (Vartanova 2012; Voltmer 2013b).

Admittedly, balance between public and private concerns about media regulation is hard to achieve in new or old democracies. Different models of media regulation are closely linked to historical or global trends, continual technological changes (the rise of social media, for instance), political turmoil or market's development. But media regulation (or the lack of it) touches every aspect of the state-media relation: ownership, funding, licensing, access, market share, contents, audiences. This is why the call is to start the political-media complex through an analysis of the state and process of media regulation.

This stance pursues at least three goals. First, to have a clearer picture about the regulatory trends among transitional democracies. With the fall of the old political regimes (authoritarianism or totalitarian rules) and as a first step towards a reconfiguration of the state-media relation, almost every transitional democracy modified its regulatory frameworks molding this interaction in more than one aspect.

Second, these first impulses for new regulatory frameworks (or the lack of them) are useful to identify the extent and scope of media regulation, as well as its consequences. This does not mean that the regulations put forward actually enabled new models of media governance in the name of democracy and the public good. Nevertheless, these processes serve as indicators of the relation that both the state and the media were pursuing at the outset of these new political regimes in significant benefit for (or perhaps in frankly detriment of) the public interest.

Third, the way in which both set of actors embrace (or not) these regulatory processes serve to complement the analysis of a set of regulatory proscriptions with common understandings, values and shared beliefs about the purpose and benefits of (or risks about) regulation. After all, what is written in laws (old or new) become meaningful through interpretation (Black 2002) and through the links that these common beliefs establish between rules and behaviour (March and Olsen 2004, 2009). Admittedly, a clear picture of the linkages between rules and actions is actually problematic (Christensen and Rovik 1999; Sending 2002; Goldmann 2005). Nevertheless, pointing at the resistances and challenges both set of actors (politicians and the media) face when translating formal rules into new practices adds elements to the analysis beyond the catastrophic image about the failure of transitional democracies to reshape their relation with media through regulation.

Paving the Road to Set the Media Free?

Generally speaking, the present state of media regulation in transitional democracies is indeed quite demoralising. Coming back to the Mexican example, the first PAN administration (President Fox 2000–2006) did embrace a regulatory process that touched key aspects of the state-media relation: structure and functioning (competition, funding, ownership); access to governmental information and public advertising. Nevertheless, Mexican researchers and practitioners have approached these reforms quite critically as hard evidence of the new democratic regime's lack of commitment to definitely end an era of cosy relations with media moguls (see for instance: Esteinou and Alva de la Selva 2009; Bravo *et al.* 2011; Trejo Delarbre and Vega Montiel 2011; Guerrero 2009). Firstly, the legal framework inherited by authoritarian rule was a complex set of entangled and outdated statutory regulations that did not respond to the new political conditions. Secondly, media moguls kept a key role in policy-making as they made extensive use of the political and economic resources at their disposal to protect their economic interests. Thirdly, news coverage also continued to be a key resource exchangeable for deference and various forms of protection for tangled economic and political interests between the new governing elites and the media (Vaca 2015).

A similar sense of regulatory failure is easily extended to other Latin American countries. Weak regulation of the private sector that practically endorses media's concentration and political clientelism (Hallin and Papathanassopoulos 2002) keeps being the Achilles' heel of the region (Guerrero and Márquez-Ramírez 2014). The cases of Venezuela, Bolivia and Ecuador certainly do not help to reconsider the capacity that Latin American states do preserve to use media policy as a handy mechanism of control and repression (see for instance: Quintanilla 2015; Kitzberger 2012; Lugo-Ocando and Romero 2000). Some emerging (limited yet fruitful) efforts to support community media in Brazil, El Salvador and Chile might bring some hope. But these isolated efforts to strengthen civic participation in the name of the public interest have not been able to revert the savage media commercialisation that actually precedes the democratisation process (Araya 2014; Matos 2015; Albuquerque 2012). Writing about the role of the state in Brazilian media during the 1980s and 1990s, Albuquerque (2012: 86) points out: 'In contrast to what happened in Europe and in many countries around world, [. . .] there was no place for a "commercial deluge" simply because Brazilian media already had a commercial character'. The assertion applies to other Latin American countries. In an effort to address the challenges that new technologies impose over the industry (digital convergence, alternative platforms, audience fragmentation *vs.* market concentration, globalisation) new regulatory frameworks in the region have ended up strengthening big media conglomerates that emerged (and remain) closely linked to the political power.

An intertwined relation between the political power and the structure or functioning of the media through media regulation also characterised post-soviet transitional democracies in Eastern Europe. But the logic behind the state interference and its control mechanisms were quite different from the ones used in Latin America. Rather than 'media capture' where big conglomerates imposed great influence on the state-media relation (like in the Latin American experience), the notions of 'colonisation of the media' stresses the role that political parties and state media have had on the configuration of media systems in Central and Eastern Europe. Two aspects are key in this process: (1) the management of information by state media, and; (2) a non-transparent political control over both state and private media (Bajomi-Lázár 2013). That is, in terms of regulation, the colonisation of the media implies poor regulatory frameworks combined with weak (or inexistent) enforcement. 'Contradictions among media-related laws and constitutions and international obligations', informs UNESCO (2014: 8) in a recent regional report about trends in freedom of expression and media, 'have underscored the continuing challenges to media freedom'. The prospects of EU membership brought some innovative regulatory frameworks envisioned to protect the public interest, but this impulse was short (Stetka 2012). Towards the second half of the 2010s, different international organisations ranked most of the EU's Eastern members below their Western partners in terms of media freedom (Freedom House 2015, Behmer 2009). Behind the veil of media policy, political parties (especially single-party governments) have turned party patronage and clientelism into media instrumentalisation (Krygier 2015; Mungiu-Pippidi 2013).

For their part, transitional democracies in Africa present a quite different story. Generally speaking, against what it is happening in the Europe (new and old democracies), 'when people are asked what public institutions they trust the most', writes White (2008: 283 paraphrasing to Bratton *et al.* 2005: 229), 'the national broadcasting services got the highest rating'. This might not come as a surprise if one takes into consideration that in sharp contrast to Latin American media but similarly to what happened in the Soviet rule, the largest and best-equipped broadcasting networks in Africa during the authoritarian rule were (and still are) owned by the state (White 2008: 315). This is not to deny the role that private (mainly international conglomerates) and locally owned entrepreneurial complexes do have in African print and broadcasting. But, generally speaking, this rather limited private and commercial media remain close tide to the ruling elites (Blankson 2007). This tendency goes way back to the colonial times, when the ruling empires invested on developing media outlets (first print and then broadcasting) for exporting media structures, formats and contents to their territories, rather than for strengthening local publications or adapting broadcasting to indigenous needs and practices. In the first decades of independence, the new governments regarded the media as handy instruments to preserve national unity and promote development. State-owned media was thus the natural course to follow. Official control over the media, intolerance to critical journalism and frequent harassment to freedom of expression was a common denominator for the authoritarian and military rules in the continent. The process of democratisation did bring few media outlets independent from government. But the presence of the African states as owner of and as one of the main investors on the media remains (Hadland 2012; Stremlau and Gagliardone 2015).

Vague Rationale Underpinning Media Laws

Approaching media regulation (less or more) as a measurement of democracy is, however, problematic. In the Mexican case, for instance, even when media regulation did generate an intense debate among diverse actors and received ample news coverage, two aspects that characterised media policy in the authoritarian rule did remain throughout the democratic transition. Lack of clarity about the rationale of media regulation and a weak rational legal authority dissolves operational links between rules, the willingness to follow them and the functional enforcement mechanisms to guarantee the protection of the public interest transcending particular interests (Vaca 2015). That is, by themselves, the new laws (debatably good or bad) did not automatically changed the perception about the uses and general responses from citizens, politicians or the media to media regulation. In the end, rather than overturning past regulatory practices and conceptions about the rationale and value of media regulation, the media regulatory framework in place at the outset of the Mexican democracy (old and new regulations) perpetuated informal responses that had the effect of limiting the significance of what the new norms proscribed.

Something similar happened in other Latin American countries. That is, the 'new' democratically elected governing elites in the region keep using media regulation as an instrument for upholding the industry at close complicity. The power that the state or the media have to control this interaction varies across the region. The range of experiences is actually ample: from (apparently) almighty media moguls such as the Mexican Televisa or the Brazilian Globo, to controlling political regimes that hamper the media (in Venezuela, Ecuador, Bolivia and Argentina, for instance). In any case, a cautious analysis of the new media regulations in the region points to the scope of these regulatory frameworks (high or low) and also to the extent of which these new regulations differ from previous ones in terms of the mechanisms and the instruments the state (or the industry) have to control the politics-media relation throughout regulation. The degree of state intervention on the structure and functioning of the media through regulation remains high in Latin America. What the process of democratisation has changed is this kind of intervention. Certainly, it is not repressive (like during the military rules in Argentina, Chile or the Brazilian *Estado Novo*) or direct through licensing (like in the early years of the Mexican, Colombian or Bolivian broadcasting). But behind poor and weak media regulation for new technologies and convergence processes, the interests of powerful media moguls that have managed to remain closely linked to (new and old) political actors prevail.

In Central and Eastern Europe, poor implementation undermines highly crafted media laws (UNESCO 2014). 'For implementation, it is often forgotten', contends Krygier (2015: 129), 'also depends upon the disposition of the implementees'. New laws in the region, as they might have been envisioned in the early years of the post-communist era, did not overcome strong clientelistic networks that misinterpreted and misused statutory legislation (Jakubowicz and Sükösd 2008). In this line of reasoning, Belakova and Tarlea (2013: 5) find that the volatility of media legislation in the region responds to three absences: (1) a general misunderstanding among decision-makers about media issues; (2) the lack of a clear conceptual and systemic vision about media policy as a mechanism to enhance the role of the media in the process of democratisation, and; (3) nonexistent long-term strategies to support the development of a healthy media environment. In this sense, 'media privatization that failed to take existing power structures into account', adds Voltmer (2015: 226), 'also helped old elites to perpetuate their influence on public opinion and political decision-making'.

In Africa, the process of democratisation has not been able to break down the inertia for state-owned media. Far from enhancing independent, accountable and diverse public broadcasters (as a distinct from government mouthpieces), these arrangements serve more as barriers than vehicles for solving two recurrent challenges in the continent: (1) the scarcity of the resources (financial and human) needed to promote a diverse and grass-roots media, and; (2) a market failure in terms of what Berger (2007: 148) names 'the worst of all worlds': state-owned media that are neither account-able to nor are steered by the public interest, and which in the search of steady sources of revenue not only privilege commercial contents to bring in advertisers, but also deprive emerging small and weak private entrepre-neurs from these resources.

A Logic of 'Inappropriateness'

The analysis of media regulation in transitional democracies is indeed dis-appointing, yet it does show some value. If these laws 'have not lived up the expectation of the most enthusiastic institutional optimists', argues Krygier (2015: 133), 'they have frequently disturbed the stasis assumed by cultural pessimist'. Right after the end of the communist regime, the policy-making agenda for legislation on the media was regarded as a pro-cess of imitation of Western media policy models. Few years later, the incorporation of these new transitional democracies to the EU imposed new challenges for media regulation. Nevertheless, these two processes do not fully explain why Central and Eastern European countries have such dissimilar approaches toward media policies rationales and strategies; at the same time these countries do share certain characteristics (the colonisa-tion of the media, for instance) that set them apart from older EU members (Klimkiewicz 2010). Media regulation in the region has made evident that this process cannot be only regarded as a mechanism for regulating privati-sation and market competition, but it has also to be approached as a process where the different (and competing) political forces negotiate the influence that they retain over the media.

Similarly, media regulation in Latin American transitional democracies has made the links between politics and the media evident. In this con-text, back to the previous states of media control, repression or unveiled complicity is simply not feasible. Both politicians and the media have had to redefine their relationship. For instance, during the first years of demo-cratic rule in Mexico, the media policy-making process put forth shaped the state-media relation in some indirect and informal, yet influential ways. First, it was simply not possible for the new political regime (at least the Fox administration) to ignore or postpone an intense debate about media regulation, as authoritarian rule did it for decades. Second, the challenges to translate formal rules into new practices and behaviour that corresponded to the new democratic setting became evident not just in regards to the highly-contested initiatives, but also in the much celebrated ones (as the transparency law, for instance). Third, rather than overturning past regula-tory practices and conceptions about the rationale and value of media regu-lation, the media regulatory framework in place (old and new regulations) perpetuated informal responses that had the effect of limiting the significance (positive or negative) of what the new regulations proscribed.

In Africa, Hydén and Leslie (2002: 12–13) identify how, even when media regulatory processes are still highly controlled by the state, independent and private African media have gained some terrain by offering distinct and alternative fora for debating media regulation issues.

As argued in the political-media complex, one will not learn much about media regulation in transitional democracies by looking at the laws and regulatory mechanisms by their own. 'For law to matter', writes Krygier (2015: 131), 'people must care or at least worry about what the law says, the rules themselves must be taken seriously, and the institutions must come to matter'. If one has to name one key common element into the divergent and even contradictory media regulatory processes in the transitional democracies, broadly reviewed is the fact that 'people do care' about media regulation. There are, naturally, very dissimilar explanations about why or what for 'people' (governing elites, political parties, congress people, media moguls, journalists) 'care' about media laws. An analysis of media regulation that takes into consideration the rationales (legal, economic or political) behind media regulation brings some light about the different aspects at stake in these processes, especially about formal and informal processes that work for or against these laws.

Admittedly, assessing the impact of regulatory frameworks on the state-media relation is far from being a straightforward task. Many aspects (the state's capacity and willingness to enhance regulation, media's influence on policy-making, the rational legal authority that supports regulation, to mention some) are at stake. Plus, a sense of imminent failure surrounds the analysis. Lack of political will, vaguely formulated laws, 'toothless' regulatory frameworks aiming at protecting the interests of powerful media moguls, laws that attempt to restrict hostile media, poor implementation or too strong or too weak regulators, are all latent dangers to transitional democracies.

Why then study the state-media relation through media policy? First, to have a better picture of the dilemmas embedded on this process. Media moguls 'capture' media policy in Latin America; political parties 'colonise' it in Central and Eastern Europe, while African states do retain a potential capacity of controlling the process. But differences among and especially within regions do shed some light about the scope and both the state and the medias' role in enabling (or not) an environment for media independence, whether it is from the controls of the state, the market or other particular interests as opposed to the public good. Second, media legislation is anything but a homogenous and unidirectional process. Diversity of meanings surrounding media regulation also denotes divergences about political will, capacity of implementation and enforcement, coherence, as well as clarity about the objectives and mechanism of these regulatory processes. Third, what it is written in the laws too often clashes with what it is actually happening. The content of media laws might be the result of meaningful consultations and negotiations, but the result is still not necessarily more democracy.

Box 4.1   Media Regulation From the Political-Media Complex Perspective

- What for?
- How?
- With what consequence(s)?

Organisational Functioning: Resistances to Change?

The second element under scrutiny proposed in the political-media complex is the organisational dynamic. 'A media system as such', write Rantanen and Belakova (2015: 311), 'cannot democratize societies if they are undemocratic'. But a key challenge of approaching the state-media relation from this perspective is that the dimension of organisational structure and daily functioning is too common approached as a 'black box': 'something' occurs inside political parties, offices of government communication, news rooms or media's executive boards that it inevitably moulds the relationship between politics and the media. Researchers thus need to be cautious when claiming that the failure in achieving the expectations imposed by the change from authoritarianism to democracy is, to a great extent, explained by organisational factors such as the production of the news, journalists' roles, the functioning of government communication offices or the actual existence of formal and informal practices connecting both sets of actors. Investigating what exactly is going on inside politics and the media that imposes such a great influence in the state-media relation requires detailed analyses on the structure and functioning of these set of actors.

The political-media complex proposes to focus the analysis at this level on three aspects: (1) organisational charts; (2) practices and day-to-day routines; (3) measures of public response and evaluation procedures. Here the call is for more empirical evidence coming from comparative research. The current understanding of these aspects in transitional (and old) democracies remains incomplete and provisional at least for three reasons.

First, empirical data is dispersed among different areas of study of media and politics. Particularly in the last two decades there has been a considerable amount of research done on news production from different perspectives (political economy, sociology, roles or cultural constraints on news work, for instance). But relatively little of it pays attention to structural and financial resources that media organisations invest (hierarchy, funding, wages, editorial and news-gathering services available) for liberal democratic models of journalism to take root far from Western democracies (Hanitzsch 2007). Journalism does not take the same form from country to country (Weaver 1998; Hallin and Mancini 2004a; Nerone 2012). There is a considerable corpus of work drawing on a range of normative approaches to journalism (Christians *et al.* 2009) from the individual level of analysis (Preston 2009).

Yet, relatively few comparative studies have paid attention to functional and structural resources (Lowrey 2009) that also shape the way in which journalists conduct their job on day-to-day basis (Esser 2013; Becker and Tudor Vlad 2009; Hanitzsch and Donsbach 2012).

Second, what it is known about what happens inside the media (in newsrooms for instance), greatly contrasts with what it is known about how political actors manage their relation with the media on regular basis (be it government communication offices or political parties' political communication war rooms). When looking at communication processes that come from political actors, research (substantially political communication) has been concentrated on political campaigning, rather than on how the regular course of government communication evolves once candidates arrive to public offices (for few exceptions see: Scammell 1995; Kurtz 1998). Government communication, stress Canel and Sanders (2012: 85), 'is an under-researched area of political communications studies, finding itself in a kind of theoretical no-man's land between political communication, public relations and organizational communication research'. As a promising area of studies, government communication contributes to a better understanding of the state-media relation in general and in particular, about the goals and tactics used in political communication. Scholarship in this topic, however, remains trapped in a paradox (Rivers *et al.* 1975): there are a large amount of studies on the government—public administration, elections, public institutions and characteristics of government officials and their performance—, while media studies has developed mainly as a rich interdisciplinary field (see for instance: Bräuchler and Postill 2010; Gray and Lotz 2012; Couldry and Hepp 2013). Nevertheless, there is relatively too little comparative research on government communication able to shed some light about the influence it poses on the state-media relation.

Third, the process of understanding how journalist or political communicators behave has a double face. On one side, assuming to be a universal model of journalism or political campaigning is becoming more and more simplistic and naïve. On the other, the role of citizens in these processes is becoming more difficult to trace. Current literature on the state-media relation in new democracies lack conceptualisations and analytical tools able to explain what is the role that citizens (or consumers) play in moulding the interaction between politics and the media. Some hope is endowed to the new platforms, communication technologies and recent changes in the media environment that allow citizens to participate directly on the political debate (Deibert and Rohozinski 2010; Christensen 2011; Dahlgren and Alvares 2013; Dalton 2013; Couldry 2015). But this era of 'media abundance' that has a direct impact on how messages are produced, distributed and consumed also imposes multiple vectors of influence over these fairly new democracies: at times strengthening democratic transition, while at other times making it even more difficult to democracy to take permanent roots (Voltmer and Sorensen 2016: 1). The role that citizens play in both journalism and political communication need better analyses able to trace how political elites, media and ordinary citizens interact in the transformation of public communication since the empirical evidence points at diverse and ambivalent experiences (see for instance: Jebril *et al.* 2013; Voltmer 2013b; Zielonka 2015).

Box. 4.2 Organisational Dynamic: Opening a Pandora's Box

• Empirical data dispersed among different areas of study
• Disparity between analyses on the media (newsrooms) and on politics (day-to-day government communication, campaigning war rooms)
• Difficulties to trace the role of citizens (or consumers) in the transformation of the politics-media relation

---

Change and Continuities: Trapped Into the Past or Moving Forward?

Inevitably, but generally overlooked by normative approaches or ideal-type categorisations, the interaction between politics and the media in transitional democracies is a product of both provoked change and fostered continuity. In few words, the state-media relation at the outset of transitional regimes was not a blank slate on which the politicians and the media freely established new (arguably more democratic) relationships.

To assess this interplay between change and continuity, the political-media complex proposes to look closely at the 'professionalisation of political communication' (Mancini 1999; Negrine 2007; Gibson and Römmele 2009;

Strömbäck 2009; Sanders *et al.* 2011). As seen in Chapter 3, this stance allows tracking how political communication is claimed to be different from the past through specialisation and displacement (Scammell 1997). This perspective adds to the structural factors in the analysis the possibility to look at individual level's characteristics and trends. That is, the state-media relation is gradually, cumulatively and incrementally transformed by the change of political regime, but also by the growth of specialised knowledge and techniques at the individual level linked to the newly introduced communication technologies and an increasing influence of the media in communicating politics. At the same time, however, this constant process of change is ultimately, subtly and thoroughly reconfigured by certain capacity and agency that political actors and the media (especially in transitional democracies) deliberatively and purposely retrain to perpetuate the role of past practices, old actors and traditional channels in communicating about politics.

In the political-media complex, this process of professionalisation represents thus an 'overarching approach' (Negrine 2007: 31) to trace the growth of specialised knowledge and techniques which is triggered by the newly introduced media technologies and platforms coupled with new but also old political communication practices. Figure 4.1 serves as a snapshot of a fluent and interrelated process of change that occurs simultaneously in politics, the media and citizens that at the same time influences the way in which politics is communicated.

Changes in politics can broadly be seen through adjustments (or even radical transformations) in the political system or more specific changes in political parties such as the emergence of 'catch all' parties or the increasing influence and role that the personal image of the candidates plays in defining the course of politics.

The secularisation of politics describes, for instance, a trend of change whereby traditional patterns of public information and civic participation are replaced by more individualistic forms of social engagement and thus of political communication (Swanson and Mancini 1996; Mazzoleni and Schulz 1999). From this stance, it becomes possible to trace the emergence of 'catch-all' parties and the decline of partisanship and voting turnout, coupled with increasing numbers of independent candidates, single-issued associations, non-governmental organizations or protest movements. As a result, traditional partisan ties between citizens and politicians weaken, while other forms of social organisation emerge. Non-governmental organisations and voluntary associations, for instance, progressively replace some of the key functions that political parties have traditionally played in society such as being a forum for public debate or function as key channels of representation and public participation (see for instance: Dogan 1997;

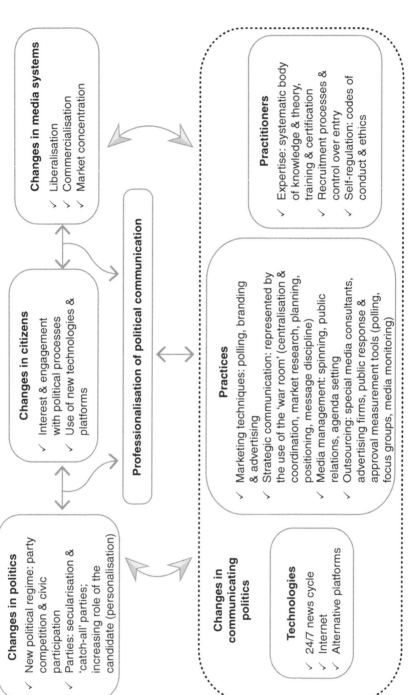

Changes in media systems

- ✓ Liberalisation
- ✓ Commercialisation
- ✓ Market concentration

Changes in citizens

- ✓ Interest & engagement with political processes
- ✓ Use of new technologies & platforms

Changes in politics

- ✓ New political regime: party competition & civic participation
- ✓ Parties: secularisation & 'catch-all' parties; increasing role of the candidate (personalisation)

Professionalisation of political communication

Practitioners

- ✓ Expertise: systematic body of knowledge & theory, training & certification
- ✓ Recruitment processes & control over entry
- ✓ Self-regulation: codes of conduct & ethics

Practices

- ✓ Marketing techniques: polling, branding & advertising
- ✓ Strategic communication: represented by the use of the 'war room' (centralisation & coordination, market research, planning, positioning, message discipline)
- ✓ Media management: spinning, public relations, agenda setting
- ✓ Outsourcing: special media consultants, advertising firms, public response & approval measurement tools (polling, focus groups, media monitoring)

Changes in communicating politics

Technologies

- ✓ 24/7 news cycle
- ✓ Internet
- ✓ Alternative platforms

Figure 4.1 The Professionalisation of Political Communication: An Overarching Approach

Dalton and Wattenberg 2000; Kitschelt 2000). Thus, secularisation processes confront both politicians and the news media with new realities such as the kind and amount of political information audiences are expecting, the support or attention that political actors actually receive from citizens and the diversity of actors participating in the political debate (Swanson 1997, 2004; Hallin and Mancini 2004b).

'The developments of political communication', write Esser and Pfetsch (2004: 12), 'thus mark the consequences of a fundamental transformation in society which has changed the three integral coordinates of the communication system—political actors, media, and the public'. These transformations are visible all over the world. 'In their products, in their professional practices and cultures, in their systems of relationships with other social institutions', as Hallin and Mancini (2004b: 25) put it, 'media systems are becoming increasingly alike. Political systems, meanwhile, are becoming increasingly similar in the patterns of communication they incorporate'.

Nevertheless, comparative research on media systems shows that national contexts do influence the way in which political communication changes around the world. On this view, social and political changes do acquire diverse forms and bring distinctive consequences that are directly related to specific contextual and indigenous aspects. For instance, the extent to which citizens remain attentive to the political process and even become active participants in the public debate varies according to particular cultural, contextual and specific national adaptation strategies in communicating politics (Bennett and Entman 2001). New information and communication technologies, the secularisation of politics and the commercialisation of public information occur in a context of other socio-political and economic changes that are both propellers of and constraints for the new technologies and communication practices to thrive.

That is, new technologies and ongoing social and political changes have traditionally been the motors of change in the interaction between politics and the media, and thus in communicating politics to citizens. The analytical tools used to assess this complex interaction should then be useful to distinguish between the *what* that this is perpetually changing and adapting to new technologies and innovative communication practices from the *why* and *how* these forces drive politicians and the media to transform their relation (Scammell 1997: 17).

For instance, looking at the key changes in politics in Central and Eastern Europe transitional democracies, Mancini (2015) points to high levels of political volatility (short life of political parties; continuous replacement of governments; lack of political expertise from the new governing cadres; fragility and instability) as key determinants of the way the media are organised and function on daily bases at least for three reasons: (1) continuous changes in professional routines attempting to adapt to constant changes in the political elites; (2) a lack of certainty about regulation policies; (3) the use of informal mechanisms to overcome this volatility and uncertainty.

In contrast, populist governments in Latin America (in Venezuela, Bolivia or Ecuador, for instance) are expected to regain and sustain a strong dominance in the generation of public policies. The process whereby public debate takes place and is transformed into public policies is characterised by strong and strident political leaders that arbitrarily take the course of public policies and impose almost a mythical sense to the 'public good' resulting on highly personalistic and hegemonic policies. In this scenario, other actors' room of maneuver is very limited. Political communication is thus used as a tool of control and state domination. Nevertheless, as Cañizález (2015: 174) stresses for the Venezuelan case, 'this model of communication was effective in controlling the media, but failed in handling the audiences'. That is, this 'new populism' in Latin America—highly personalistic, plebiscitary and anti-institutionalist politics—struggles to get some balance between governability and freedom; between democracy and hegemonic communication policies that aim at regaining state's control over the media and at restraining press freedom and public debate.

For their part, media systems are also in a constant process of adaptation to new conditions such as technological developments, the liberalisation of markets, competition among different media platforms and concentration of media ownership. From this stance, media, however, are not seen as mere channels of communication between politicians and citizens. They also adapt their functioning to simultaneous changes in politics. At the same time, the way in which this set of actors perform and present the news impacts the course and practice of politics.

Citizens (or consumers) also play a key part in this ever-going process of change. Changes in technologies, politics and the media bring about changes in the way citizens engage with political processes and use (consume) media technologies to get the information they need about politics. Researchers debate about the extent to which citizens are (at all) taking part in politics be it through traditional means (party alliance, voting or participating on the public debate) or by using new communication technologies and media platforms (see for instance: Chambers and Costain 2000; Fenton and Downey 2003; Jenkins *et al.* 2003; Dahlgren 2005; Habermas 2006; Castells 2008). The concept of professionalisation as proposed here in the political-media complex also allows researchers to assess transformations on the ways citizens engage (or not) in politics by linking citizens' participation to both changes in politics and the media.

As a consequence, but also as a cause of this ongoing process of change, communicating politics appears inextricably bound up with the emergence of new technologies and the increasing use of private sector communication practices and skills. Practitioners adapt their communication tactics to new communication platforms, practices and resources (human and financial) to achieve highly crafted communication strategies and goals. From this stance, academic literature places emphasis on the risks involved in this process: from citizens transformed into mere armchair consumers of politics (Herman 2003; McNair 2005; Gaber 2007), to tailored communication campaigns that privilege the drama about political life over the substance of democracy such as deliberation, representation and inclusive policy-making (Gitlin 1991; Cappella and Jamieson 1997; Sparks and Tulloch 2000; Price *et al.* 2002).

To some extent, the interrelated developments pictured in Figure 4.1 are visible all over the world. 'Professionalization', write Papathanassopoulos and his colleagues (Papathanassopoulos *et al.* 2007: 14), 'cuts across equally contested concepts such as modernization, Americanization, homogenization, as it deals with a more general process of change taking place in contemporary societies'. Depending on the focus and the emphasis that research places on the causes or consequences of these common and simultaneous transformations, academics refer to different processes (global homogenisation patterns, modernisation or the contested, yet useful notion of Americanisation) to summarise the ways in which political communication evolves.

Admittedly, existing research on these processes (professionalisation, Americanisation and even modernisation) has primarily emerged from Western democracies. Applying them to transitional democracies opens the opportunity to question the assumption about the transformative power or progressive development embedded in these concepts. Rather than seeing them as inexorable trends of transformation, they are here approached as a combination of change and stasis with unforeseen outcomes (Voltmer and Sorensen 2016: 10). Plus, recognising the array of influences that authoritarianism imposed over new democracies is a window onto the dynamics of a process of adaptation rather than of the radical transformation commonly expected in newly democracies. The goal is thus, to have a better notion as to how interrelated changes in politics, the news media and in communicating politics interact with continuities product of authoritarian legacies or path dependences.

To sum up, the political-media complex casts doubt on the utility of accounts about the professionalisation of political communication that, in highlighting the growth of specialised knowledge and techniques around new political conditions or newly introduced communication strategies and technologies, undermine the role that indigenous factors, past practices and traditional actors play in communicating about politics. Against the idea that a more professional political communication fully replaces old conceptions and practices, the political-media complex touches upon the indigenous barriers to global trends and modernisation patterns. This stance serves as the basis for elaborating an alternative perspective on the professionalisation of political communication in transitional democracies that also points at the resistance from both politicians and the media to break with past practices and beliefs about the value and functioning of political communication.

Conclusions

In generating models and their respective categorisations, specificity is clearly at stake. After all, studying the state-media relation (apparently) matters the most when similarities and discrepancies between different national context are analysed looking for general patterns that deliver functional categorisations. Hence the success of *Four Theories of the Press* (1956) and *Comparing Media Systems* (2004).

Nevertheless, more common than not, this kind of comparative research on the state-media relation foresees similar trends among democracies. As a preliminary trial of the political-media complex, a general look to empirical evidence coming from relatively distinctive democracies describes quite dissimilar experiences. Transitions to democracy are indeed anything but uniform. As shown in this chapter, it is almost impossible to draw generalisations about the state-media relation in such a diverse range of experiences. On the contrary, what emerges with a certain sense of clarity is the impracticability of packing all these experiences into one single media model [be it Siebert and his colleagues' Social Responsibility model (1956) embedded on an ideal progressive trend from authoritarianism to libertarianism; or Hallin and Mancini's (2004a: 306) Polarised Pluralist Model as 'the most widely applicable' media system instead of indistinctively assuming a liberal normative perspective].

In fact, Voltmer (2015) and Mancini (2015) urge to use the term 'hybridity' to describe those media systems that 'emerge from the mixture of external influence and domestic conditions, be they historical, economic or political' (Mancini 2015: 25). From this angle, hybridity becomes useful to describe certain common features in the state-media relation as the instrumentalisation of the media and clientelistic practices; informal traits that interact with formal laws and institutions, or; the foreign influence on the structure and functioning of the media.

Conclusions

> After reviewing the past attempts towards *Theories of the Press* one is no longer sure whether they cover the ideal or the real level. Obviously a new beginning must cover both, and not just to create emancipatory effects but also to join the eternal project of mass communication research: to understand the media, particularly in relation to society.
>
> Kaarle Nordenstreng, Beyond the *Four Theories of the Press* (1997)

This book ends as it began, with the firm conviction that a new research agenda is needed to move the study of the state-media relation forward. This is not an ordinary revolutionary impulse inspired by thriving new media technologies and platforms that inevitably urge for alternative perspectives. In the end, 'technology revolutions' (print, telegraph, radio, telephone, television, computer, mobile phones, internet, smart phones) are the motors of communication studies. New communication technologies and platforms force academics to reconsider our hypotheses. This book is neither another personal (yet justified) complaint against an extremely Western bias in the academic debate. To be fair, the 2010s are seeing an unparalleled effort to investigate media systems outside the usual battery of case studies from the Western world. Now (after sixty years of research), academics are (or *should be*) certain that rigid typologies of media systems cannot travel too far from where they are created (Voltmer 2012). Nor are these pages meant to be a sound complaint against normative standards that are simply unfeasible: neither the media nor politicians are purely and entirely committed to a public sphere where a great diversity of voices are heard and where all opinions are taken into consideration. Democratic rules aspire to be responsive, enhance civic participation and allow accountability. It is in the daily practice that these goals face all kind of challenges.

Nevertheless, this book is indeed a strident call for a turning point into the analysis of media systems. Instead of developing (continuously modifying or adding) pigeonhole typologies aimed at classifying the media according to fixed normative parameters, the political-media complex proposes an institutional analysis to this interaction. This alternative perspective does rests on normative aspirations that inevitably set key standards for both the state and the media: diversity, access, competition, representativeness, freedom of expression, responsibility. But the core of the proposal rests on centring the analysis on the actual functioning of the interaction between political regimes (in plural) and the media (also a plural noun). That is, instead of what the media *should be* (Siebert *et al.* 1956), the political-media complex aims at investigating what the interaction between the state and the media *is* and *does*. Naturally, as a proposal, the political media complex needs to be tested, criticised and adjusted. But the initial incursion here presented into this alternate point of entry for academic research on the state-media relation does show value. Here are some reasons why.

Flaws in Democratic Performance: Consequences vs. Causes

There is a strong sense among scholars (and practitioners too) that the state-media relation has become frankly dysfunctional and even danger-ous for any democratic rule (old or new). All over the globe, citizens show no interest on politics: they are sidelined, demotivated; the great majority do not vote, and the few that do prove pollsters to be either too optimis-tic or totally blind. Politicians lie: spin doctors sell them as if they were soap; political campaigning privileges image over political messages; dif-ferences among political parties are resumed to their names because their proposals and (in)actions are alike. Media also lie: infotainment pictures a world that at its best resembles a *telenovela*, and that at its worst exceeds the most popular zombies' mini-series; politics is covered as horse races, and horse races (or any other public event for the matter sake is) are used as political stages. In short, if one chooses the extreme position, the current state of the interactions between politics and the media represents a critical danger to democracy. But *why is this*? Placing the searchlight on the institu-tional causes—and not only on the general consequences of why the state-media relation falls short from the liberal democratic paradigm—is useful to reduce researchers' current tendency to impose high normative expecta-tions on this interaction without really explaining *how* and *why* normative (Western) standards do not fully describe it, or without clarifying if these models indeed represent an ideal benchmark around the globe.

When looking at transitional democracies, the political-media complex analysis presented here showed for instance that the challenges in terms of media regulation are not only about the regulatory measures and legal frameworks needed (thinking, for instance, on the contrast between public service or commercial media) or about the actors and interests involved.

Implementation, enforcement, as well as informal mechanisms and practices related to the rationale and the legal authority of these frameworks constrain the extend and scope of media regulation. From this stance, the ambiguous authority of formal rules became evident. That is, a state-media relation that at first glance could have been transformed through the enactment of new statutory regulations for the media and about political communication, remains constrained by different roles that media and political interests play on policy-making. Divergent understandings about the beneficiaries, the purpose and the scope of media regulation also play a key role on this process. When thinking on terms of democratic performance, the flaws are then not only related to the lack of (or excessive) media regulation, but also to the purpose, rationales (common understandings, values, shared beliefs) and resistances coming from different actors.

Freedom From the State, Yet Not Complete Independence

The persistent interdependence between the governing elites and media conglomerates in transitional democracies is difficult to account from normative approaches to the state-media relation. Nevertheless, the institutional lenses proposed in the political-media complex showed that politics and the media are intertwined in more than one way and at different levels. Media regulation, political communication or news management are the natural arenas where politicians and media representatives interact. But newsrooms, political campaigning war rooms and government communication offices are linked together also at the individual level when, for instance, sharing skills, personnel and professional backgrounds.

Admittedly, the appeal to approach the state-media relation as an interdependent interaction is not exclusive to the political-media complex. Other analytical approaches assessing the relationship between politics and the media in general, or politicians and journalists in particular have also stressed numerous links that tie these two set of actors together (i.e., Blumler and Gurevitch 1975, 1995; Gunther and Mughan 2000a; Hallin and Mancini 2004a; Ross 2010). But the analysis here presented points to both confrontation (tangled interests, manipulation, struggle for power, resistance) as well as to cooperation (mediation, mutual needs, reliance). From this stance, the idyllic image of a fierce watchdog ready to attack when the intruder trespass might be replaced, albeit not so easily, by a familiar notion of friendly team players that, depending on the game's strategy, could turn into aggressive contenders.

Opening 'Black Boxes'

When placing the searchlight on transitional democracies (see Chapter 4), the political-media complex gives the possibility to investigate aspects of the state-media relation that are typically relegated to the shadows. As seen in this book these are: (1) diversity of influences in which the authoritarian past shaped the state-media relation in the democratic setting; (2) the role of informal arrangements and practices in this interaction; (3) an interplay between change and continuity.

The first concerns the need to recognise that 'inertia-based explanations are insufficient' (Hite and Cesarini 2004: 326). Crucial differences among transitional democracies are, naturally, about divergent current democratic institutions, actors and dynamics. As seen, these regimes constitute a heterogeneous group that hardly fits into rigid categorisations. Understanding the role that the authoritarian past imposes over the new democratic setting is going beyond asserting that there is a deterministic relationship between the past and the present (Voltmer 2013a: 222) or assuming that it is simply more difficult for democracy to take root in post-authoritarian governments. It is, on the contrary, acknowledging that authoritarianism in transitional democracies is not a single or unidirectional (positive or negative) force. The past marks (shapes, constrains or facilitates) the present in a variety of ways: through archaic formal arrangements such as laws, policies or rigid administrative structures; through prevailing actors associated with the authoritarian regime, and; through traditional practices and past experiences, for mentioning some key aspects.

The second is more abstract. Informal arrangements (common knowledge, beliefs, attitudes and day-to-day practices) is perhaps less evident, but equally relevant to the study of the state-media relation. For instance, it cannot simply be assumed that proscriptions on the relationship between the state and the media (statutory media regulation, formal rules and written norms) always dictate the behaviour of those involved. Beliefs, attitudes and common practices are also relevant to disentangle the links between rules and actions. Similarly, budgets, organisational charts and strategic communications blueprints set certain parameters for both politicians and media representatives. But it is wrong to expect that these can be implemented without hesitation. Routines, practices and understandings about the purpose and value of the politics-media relation do shape this interaction.

Third, in the political-media complex change and continuity are complementary forces. In the study of transitional democracies the significance of this is that change does not resemble the transformation prescribed in the liberal democratic paradigm. Nor did the continuities from the past match the traditional practices and beliefs that authoritarianism used to keep media at close complicity. That is, the study of both transformation and stasis matters because, more common than not, the continuities seen might also be approached as an indication of change at different levels.

Lack of an Overreaching Framework

The state-media relation in transitional democracies shows a full range of dissimilar experiences: while in certain regions of the world media conglomerates display their influence in politics and economic power to keep (capture, manipulate) political elites at close complicity (like in Latin America), in others politicians 'colonise' the media (Rantanen and Belakova 2015) in a permanent effort of retaining control over information, socialisation, mass communication and (perhaps equally relevant) over a thriving entertainment and advertising industries (like in Eastern Europe). But thinking about politics and the media relationships constricted to national boundaries is problematic. The state might keep representing a useful analytical tool for media systems categorisations. In practice, however, the notion of homogeneity embedded in the conception of the state defies cultural and political divergences that do shape the structural and agency-related influence that media have in politics. At the same time, macro-regional economic and political constellations influence the course of the state and the media (like the EU for Central and Eastern Europe). In short, the particular characteristics of politics and media both within and without geographical borders deserve more attention.

In this context, the political-media complex serves as a unifying conceptual framework to assess the difference among and within political regimes, as well as among different media outlets. As seen, a rich amount of studies point to crucial divergences and, perhaps more interesting, key challenges media systems in transitional democracies are facing. Nevertheless, this literature lacks from a single analytical prism able to offer a better understanding of these differences. Plus, there is very little research that explores how the new political regime shape the role of the media. When the searchlight covers the new governing and political cadres, the focus tends to be on political campaigning during electoral processes (Strömbäck and Kaid 2008; Tworzecki 2012). Day-to-day government communication processes and strategies are commonly relegated to the shadows (Vaca 2015). The political-media complex might assist to recognise the relevance of endogenous and exogenous forces, approaching them with certain organisation.

It is from this stance that the task of moving the study of the relationship between political regimes and media systems forward becomes evident. It is difficult, however, to draw solid conclusions about the political-media complex from the initial tryout done in this book. It is most likely that substantial adjustments will be needed when using it in to explore detailed case-studies. Plus, the analysis of an ample range of political regimes will bring additional insights and, perhaps most relevant, may tell a cautionary story about the prospects for advancing the understanding about the functioning of democracy where the analysis of the relationship between politics and media is constrained to pigeonhole categorisations and models that (quite unintended) end up being rigid typologies and most worrying, continuously imposing certain normative aspirations about the state-media relation that, worldwide, are simply beyond reach.

References

Agee, Warren K., Phillp H. Ault, and Edwin Emery. 1994. *Introduction to mass communication*. 11th ed. New York: Harper Collins.

Albuquerque, Alfonso. 2012. On models and margins: Comparative media models viewed from a Brazilian perspective. In *Comparing media systems beyond the Western world*, edited by Daniel Hallin and Paolo Mancini, 72–96. Cambridge: Cambridge University Press.

Alexander, Gerard. 2001. Institutions, path dependence and democratic consolidation. *Journal of Theoretical Politics* 13(3): 249–270.

Almond, Gabriel A., and Sidney Verba. 1963. *The civic culture: Political attitudes in five nations*. Princeton: Princeton University Press.

Altheide, David, and Robert Snow. 1979. *Media logic*. Beverly Hills: Sage.

Altschull, J. Herbert. 1984. *Agents of power: The role of the news media in human affairs*. London: Longman.

Araya, Rodrigo. 2014. The global notion of journalism: A hindrance to democratization of the public space in Chile. In *Media systems and communication policies in Latin America*, edited by Manuel Alejandro Guerrero and Mireya Márquez-Ramírez, 245–271. Hampshire: Palgrave MacMillan.

Bajomi-Lázár, Peter. 2013. From political propaganda to political marketing: Changing patterns of political communication in Central and Eastern Europe. In *Media transformations in the post-communist world: Eastern Europe's tortured path to change*, edited by Peter Gross and Karol Jakubowicz, 49–66. Lanham, MD: Lexington Books.

Becker, Jonathan. 2004. Lessons from Russia: A neo-authoritarian media system. *European Journal of Communication* 19(2): 139–163.

Becker, Lee, and Tudor Vlad. 2009. News organizations and routines. In *The handbook of journalism studies*, edited by Karin Wahl-Jorgensen and Thomas Hanitzsch, 59–72. London: Routledge.

Behmer, Markus. 2009. Measuring media freedom: Approaches of international comparison. In *Press freedom and pluralism in Europe*, edited by Andrea Czepek, Melani Hellwig and Eva Nowak, 23–44. Bristol/Chicago: Intellect Books.

Belakova, Nikola, and Silvana Tarlea. 2013. How national parliaments legislate the media in CEE: The adoption and implementation of media legislation in the Czech Republic, Romania and Slovakia: Media Legislation fieldwork report. *Media and*

Democracy in Central and Eastern Europe Research Project. http://mde.politics. ox.ac.uk/images/stories/documents/mdcee%20legislative%20report_ro-cz-sk_ pv.pdf [last accessed: March 2017].

Bennett, Andrew, and Colin Elman. 2006. Qualitative research: Recent developments in case study methods. *Annual Review of Political Science* 9: 455–476.

Bennett, W. Lance. 1988. *News, the politics of illusion*. 2nd ed. New York: Longman.

———. 1990. Toward a theory of press-state relations in the United States. *Journal of Communication* 40(2): 103–127.

Bennett, W. Lance, and Robert M. Entman. 2001. *Mediated politics: Communication in the future of democracy*. Cambridge: Cambridge University Press.

Bennett, W. Lance, Regina G. Lawrence, and Steven Livingston. 2005. *When the press fails: Political power and the news media from Iraq to Katrina*. Chicago: University of Chicago Press.

Berger, Guy. 2007. *Media legislation in Africa: A comparative legal survey*. Grahamstown: Rhodes University/UNESCO.

Bermeo, Nancy. 1992. Democracy and the lessons of dictatorship. *Comparative Politics* 24(23): 273–291.

Beumers, Birgit, Stephen C. Hutchings, and Natalia Rulyova. 2009. *Globalisation, freedom and the media after communism: The past as future*. New York: Routledge.

Bisbal, Marcelino. 2007. Los Medios en Venezuela. ¿Dónde estamos? [Where are we?] *Cuaderno Venezolano de Sociologiía* 16(4): 64–668.

Black, Julia. 2002. *Critiical reflections on regulation*. Law Department. London: London School of Economics. [Discussion Paper].

Blankson, Isaac A. 2007. Media independence and pluralism in Africa: Opportunities and challeges of democratization and liberalization. In *Negotiating democracy: Media transformations in emerging democracies*, edited by Issac A. Blankson and Patrick D. Murphy, 15–34. Albany: SUNY Press.

Blumler, Jay C., ed. 1992. *Television and the public interest*. London: Sage.

Blumler, Jay G., and Michael Gurevitch. 1975. Towards a comparative framework for political communication research. In *Political communication: Issues and strategies for research*, edited by Steven Chaffee, 165–193. Beverly Hills: Sage.

———. 1995. *The crisis of public communication*. London: Routledge.

Blumler, Jay G., and Dennis Kavanagh. 1999. The Third age of political communication: Influences and features. *Political Communication* 16(3): 209–230.

Bolaño, César. 2014. Globalization and history in Brazil: Communication, culture, and development policies at crossroads. In *Media systems and communication policies in Latin America*, edited by Manuel Alejandro Guerrero and Mireya Márque-Ramírez, 226–242. Hampshire: Palgrave MacMillan.

Boyd-Barrett, Oliver, Colin Seymour-Ure, and Jeremy Tunstall. 1977. *Studies on the press*. London: HMSO for the Royal Commission on the Press.

Braman, Sandra. 2004. Where has media policy gone? Defining the field in the twenty-first century. *Communication Law and Policy* 9(2): 153–182.

Brants, Kees. 1998. Who's afraid of infotainment? *European Journal of Communication* 13(3): 315–335.

Bräuchler, Birgit, and John Postill, eds. 2010. *Theorising media and practice*. New York/Oxford: Berghahn.

Bravo, Jorge. 2011. Gasto en comunicación social: una década de dispendio sin regulación [The cost of political communication: A decade of expenses without regulation]. In *Panorama de la comunicación en México 2011. Desafíos para la calidad y la diversidad [Overview of mass communication in Mexico 2011: Challenges in terms of quality and diversity]*, edited by Jorge Bravo, Aimée Vega Montiel and Raúl Trejo Delarbre, 53–81. México City: AMEDI/Cámara de Diputados LXI Legislatura.

Bravo, Jorge, Aimée Vega Montiel, and Raúl Trejo Delarbre. 2011. *Panorama de la comunicación en México 2011. Desafíos para la calidad y la diversidad [Overview of mass communication in Mexico 2011: Challenges in terms of quality and diversity]*. México City: AMEDI/Cámara de Diputados LXI Legislatura.

Broughton-Micova, Sarah E. 2013. *Small and resistant: Europeanization in media governance in Slovenia and Macedonia*. PhD. Diss. The London School of Economics and Political Science.

Brunsson, Nils, and Johan P. Olsen. 1997. *The reforming organization*. Bergen: Fagbokforlaget.

Butler, David, and Austin Ranney. 1992. *Electioneering: A comparative study of continuity and change*. Oxford: Oxford University Press.

Campbell, John L. 1995. Institutional analysis and the role of ideas in political economy. *Seminar on the State and Capitalism since 1800*. [Conference paper].

Canel, María José, and Karen Sanders. 2010. Para estudiar la comunicación de los gobiernos: un análisis del estado de la cuestión [For the study of government communication: An analysis on the state of the art]. *Comunicación y Sociedad* 23(1): 7–48.

———. 2012. Government communication: An emerging field in political communication research. In *The Sage handbook of political communication*, edited by Holly A. Semetko and Margaret Scammell, 85–96. London: Sage.

Canel, María José, and Kathrin Voltmer, eds. 2014. *Comparing political communication across time and space*. Hampshire: Palgrave MacMillan.

Cañizález, Andrés. 2015. The state in pursuit of hegemoy over the media: The Chávez model. In *Media systems and communication policies in Latin America*, edited by Manuel Alejandro Guerrero and Mireya Márquez-Ramírez, 245–271. Hampshire: Palgrave MacMillan.

Capoccia, Giovanni, and Daniel Kelemen. 2007. The study of critical junctures: Theory, narrative and couterfactuals in Historical Institutionalism. *World Politics* 59(3): 341–369.

Cappella, Joseph, and Kathleen Jamieson. 1997. *Spiral of cynicism: The press and the public good*. Oxford: Oxford University Press.

Capriles, Oswaldo. 1976. *El Estado y los medios de comunicación en Venezuela*. Caracas: Suma.

Castells, Manuel. 2008. The new public sphere: Global civil society, communication networks, and global governance. *The Annals of the American Academy* 616 (March): 78–93.

Chambers, Simone, and Anne N. Costain. 2000. *Deliberation, democracy, and the media*. Lanham, MD: Rowman & Littlefield Publishers.

Christensen, Christian. 2011. Discourses of technology and liberation: State aid to net activists in an era of 'twitter revolutions'. *The Communication Review* 14(3): 233–253.

Christensen, Tom, and Kjell Arne Rovik. 1999. The ambiguity of appropriateness. In *Organizing political institutions*, edited by Morten Egeberg and Per Laegreid, 159–180. Olso: Scandinavian University Press.

Christians, Clifford G., Theodore L. Glasser, Denis McQuail, Kaarle Nordenstreng, and Robert A. White. 2009. *Normative theories of the media: Journalism in democratic societies.* Urbana: University of Illinois Press.

Cook, Timothy E. 1998. *Governing with the news: The news media as a political institution.* Chicago: University of Chicago Press.

Couldry, Nick. 2015. The Myth of 'us': Digital networks, political change and the production of collectivity. *Information, Communication & Society* 18(6): 608–626.

Couldry, Nick, and Andreas Hepp. 2013. Conceptualizing mediatization: Contexts, traditions, arguments. *Communication Theory* 23(3): 191–202.

Curran, James. 1991. Rethinking the media as a public sphere. In *Communication and citizenship*, edited by Peter Dahlgren and Colin Sparks, 27–57. London: Routledge.

———. 2005. *What democracy requires of the media?* Oxford: Oxford University Press.

———. 2011. *Media and democracy.* London: Routledge.

Dahl, Robert Alan. 1989. *Democracy and its critiques.* New Haven: Yale University Press.

Dahlgren, Peter. 2005. The internet, public spheres, and political communication: Dispersion and deliberation. *Political Communication* 22(2): 147–162.

Dahlgren, Peter, and Claudia Alvares. 2013. Political participation in an age of mediatisation. *Javnost—The Public* 20(2): 47–65.

Dalton, Russell J. 2013. *Citizen politics: Public opinion and political parties in advanced industrial democracies.* 6th ed. Los Angeles: CQ Press.

Dalton, Russell J., and Martin P. Wattenberg. 2000. *Parties without partisans: Political change in advanced industrial democracies.* Oxford: Oxford University Press.

Davis, Aeron. 2002. *Public relations democracy: Public relations, politics, and the mass media in Britain.* Manchester: Manchester University Press.

———. 2009. Journalist-source relations, mediated reflexivity and the politics of politcs. *Journalism Studies* 10(2): 204–219.

Deibert, Ronald, and Rafal Rohozinski. 2010. Liberation *vs.* control: The future of cyberspace. *Journal of Democracy* 21(4): 43–57.

de la Mora, Diego. 2009. Abuso de la publicidad gubernamental [Abuses of governmental public advertising]. *Etcétera* (January): 44–52.

Delli Carpini, Michael X., and Bruce A. Williams. 2001. Let us infotain you: Politics in the new media environment. In *Mediated politics: Communication in the future of democracy*, edited by W. Lance Bennett and Robert M. Entman, 160–181. Cambridge: Cambridge University Press.

de Smaele, Hedwing. 1999. The applicability of Western media models on the Russian media system. *European Journal of Communication* 14(2): 173–189.

Diamond, Larry Jay. 2002. Thinking about hybrid regimes. *Journal of Democracy* 13(2): 21–35.

Dobek-Ostrowska, Boguslawa, Karol Jakubowicz, and Miklós Sükösd. 2010. *Comparative media systems: European and global perspectives.* Budapest: Central European University Press.

Dogan, Mattei. 1997. Erosion of confidence in advanced democracies. *Studies in Comparative International Devolopment* 32(3): 3–29.

Downey, John, and Sabina Mihelj. 2012. *Central and Eastern European media in comparative perspective: Politics, economy and culture.* Burlington: Ashgate.

Doyle, Gillian. 2002. *Understanding media economics.* London: Sage.

Dwyer, Paul. 2015. Theorizing media production: The poverty of political economy. *Media, Culture & Society* 37(7): 988–1004.

———. 2016. Understanding media production: A rejoinder to Murdock and Golding. *Media, Culture & Society* 38(8): 1272–1275.

Dyczok, Marta, and Oxana Gaman-Golutvina. 2009. *Media, democracy and freedom: The post-communist experience.* Bern: Peter Lang.

Eckstein, Harry. 1979. On the 'science' of the state. *Daedalus* 108(4): 1–20.

Elster, Jon. 1989. *The cement of society: A study of social order.* Cambridge: Cambridge University Press.

Entman, Robert M. 1989. *Democracy without citizens: Media and the decay of American politics.* Oxford: Oxford University Press.

Escobedo, Juán Francisco. 2000. *Resonancias del México autoritario [Signs of the authoritarian Mexico].* México: Universidad Iberoamericana, UNESCO, Fundación Manuel Buendía.

Esser, Frank. 2013. The emerging paradigm of comparative communication enquiry: Advancing cross-national research in times of globalization. *International Journal of Communication* 7: 113–128.

Esser, Frank, and Barbara Pfetsch, eds. 2004. *Comparing political communication.* Cambridge: Cambridge University Press.

Esteinou, Javier, and Alma Alva de la Selva. 2009. *La Ley Televisa y la lucha por el poder en México [The Televisa Law and the struggle for power in Mexico].* México: UNAM.

Feintuck, Mike, and Mike Varney. 2006. *Media regulation, public interest and the law.* 2nd ed. Edinburgh: Edinburgh University Press.

Fenton, Nancy, and John Downey. 2003. Counter public spheres and global modernity. *Javnost—The Public* 10(1): 15–32.

Fernández Christlieb, Fátima. 1982. *Los medios de difusión masiva en México [Mass communication media in Mexico].* México: Ediciones Casa Juán Pablos.

Fox, Elizabeth, and Patricia Anzola. 1998. Politics and regional television in Colombia. In *Medios and politics in Latin America: The struggle for democracy,* edited by Elizabeth Fox, 82–92. London: Sage.

Franklin, Robert. 1994. *Packing politics: Communication in Britain's media democracy.* London: Arnold.

Freedom House. 2015. Freedom of the press 2016. *The Battle for the Dominant Message.* freedomhouse.org [last accessed: March 2017].

Gaber, Ivor. 2007. Too much of a good thing: The 'problem' of political communications in a mass media democracy. *Journal of Public Affairs* 7(3): 219–234.

Gamson, William A. 1989. News as framing. *American Behavioral Scientist* 33(2): 157–161.

———. 1992. *Talking politics.* Cambridge: Cambridge University Press.

Gandy, Oscar H. 1982. *Beyond agenda setting: Information subsidies and public policy.* Norwood, NJ: Ablex.

Gans, Herbert J. 1980. *Deciding what's news: A study of CBS evening news, NBC nightly news, Newsweek and Time.* London: Constable.

———. 2003. *Democracy and the news.* New York/Oxford: Oxford University Press.

García Rubio, Claudia I. 2008. *Para entender la televisión en México [To understand Television in Mexico].* México: Fragua San Pablo.

Garnett, James L. 1997. Trends and gaps in the treatment of communication in organization and management theory. *Public Administration and Public Policy 63*: 21–60.

Garnham, Nicholas. 1990. *Capitalism and communication: Global culture and the economics of information.* London: Sage.

Geddes, Barbara. 1999. What do we know about democratization after twenty years? *Annual Review of Political Science* 2: 115–144.

Gibson, Rachel K., and Andrea Römmele. 2009. Measuring the professionalization of political campaigning. *Party Politics* 15(3): 265–293.

Gitlin, Tood. 1991. Bits and blips: Chunk news, savvy talk and bifurcation of American Politics. In *Communication and citizenship: Journalism and the public sphere*, edited by Peter Dahlgren and Colin Sparks, 117–134. London: Routledge.

Goldenberg, Edie N. 1975. *Making the papers: The access of resource-poor groups to the metropolitan press.* Lexington, MA: Lexington Books.

Goldmann, Kjell. 2005. Appropriateness and consequences: The logic of neo-institutionalism. *Governance* 18(1): 35–52.

Goodin, Robert E., and Hans-Dieter Klingemann. 1996. *A new handbook of political science.* Oxford: Oxford University Press.

Graber, Doris A. 2003. The media and democracy: Beyond myths and stereotypes. *Annual Review of Political Science* 6 (June): 139–160.

Gray, Jonathan, and Amanda D. Lotz. 2012. *Television studies.* Cambridge: Polity Press.

Gross, Peter. 2002. *Entangled evolutions: The media and democratization in Eastern Europe.* Baltimore: The Johns Hopkins University Press/Woodrow Wilson Center Press.

Gross, Peter, and Karol Jakubowicz, eds. 2013. *Media transformations in the post-communist world.* Lanham: Lexington Books.

Guedes-Bailey, Olga, and Othon F. Jambeiro Barbosa. 2008. The media in Brazil: An historical overview of Brazilian broadcasting politics. In *The media in Latin America*, edited by Jairo Lugo-Ocando, 46–60. Maidenhead: Open University Press/McGraw-Hill.

Guerrero, Manuel Alejandro. 2009. *The emergence of pluralism in Mexican broadcasting: Economics over politics.* Saarbrücken: VDM Verlag.

———. 2010a. Los medios de comunicación y el régimen político [The media and the political regime]. In *Los grandes problemas de México [The great problems of Mexico]*, edited by Manuel Ordorica and Jean François Prud'homme, 232–300. México: El Colegio de México.

———. 2010b. Broadcasting and democracy in Mexico: From corporatist subordination to state capture. *Policy and Society* 29(1): 23–35.

Guerrero, Manuel Alejandro, and Mireya Márquez-Ramírez, eds. 2014. *Media systems and communication policies in Latin America.* Hampshire: Palgrave MacMillan.

Gunaratne, Shelton A. 2010. De-Westernizing communication. *Media, Culture and Society* 32(3): 473–500.

Gunther, Richard, and Anthony Mughan, eds. 2000a. *Democracy and the media: A comparative perspective*. Cambridge: Cambridge University Press.

———. 2000b. The political impact of the media: A reassessment. In *Democracy and the media: A comparative perspective*, edited by Richard Gunther and Anthony Mughan, 402–447. Cambridge: Cambridge University Press.

Gunther, Richard, Hans-Jürgen Puhle, and Nikiforos P. Diamandouros, eds. 1995. *The politics of democratic consolidation: Southern Europe in comparative perspective*. Baltimore: The Johns Hopkins University Press.

Habermas, Jurgen. 2006. Political communication in media society: Does democracy still enjoy an epistemic dimension? The impact of normative theory on empirical research. *Communication Theory* 16(4): 411–426.

Hachten, William A. 1981. *The world news prism*. Ames: Iowa State University Press.

Hadenius, Axel, and Jan Teorell. 2006. *Authoritarian regimes: Stability, change and pathways to democracy 1972–2003*. Washington DC: The Helen Kellogg Institute for International Studies. [Working Paper].

Hadland, Adrian. 2012. Africanizing three models of media and politics. In *Comparing media systems beyond the Western world*, edited by Daniel Hallin and Paolo Mancini, 96–118. Cambridge: Cambridge University Press.

Hague, Rod, Martin Horrop, and John McCormick. 2016. *Comparative government and politics*. 10th ed. London: Palgrave MacMillan.

Hall, Peter A. 1986. *Governing the economy: The politics of state intervention in Britain and France, Europe and the international order*. Cambridge: Polity Press.

———. 2010. Historical institutionalism in rationalist and sociological perspective. In *Explaining institutional change: Ambiguity, agency, and power*, edited by James Mahoney and Kathleen Thelen, 204–223. Cambridge: Cambridge University Press.

Hall, Peter A., and Rosmeray Taylor. 1996. Political science and the three new institutionalisms. *Political Studies* 44(5): 936–957.

Hall, Stuart, Chas Critcher, Tony Jefferson, John Clarke, and Brian Roberts. 1978. *Policing the crisis: Mugging, the state, and law and order*. London: Palgrave MacMillan.

Hallin, Daniel C. 1986. *The 'uncensored war': The media and Vietnam*. Oxford: Oxford University Press.

———. 1992. Sound bite democracy. *The Wilson Quarterly* 16(2): 34–37.

Hallin, Daniel C., and Paolo Mancini. 2004a. *Comparing media systems: Three models of media and politics*. Cambridge: Cambridge University Press.

———. 2004b. Americanization, globalization and secularization: Understanding the convergence of media systems and political communication. In *Comparing political communication: Theories, cases, and challenges*, edited by Frank Esser and Barbara Pfetsch, 25–44. Cambridge: Cambridge University Press.

———, eds. 2012. *Comparing media systems beyond the Western world*. Cambridge: Cambridge University Press.

Hallin, Daniel C., and Stylianos Papathanassopoulos. 2002. Political clientelism and the media: Southern Europe and Latin America in comparative perspective. *Media, Culture & Society* 24(2): 175–195.

Hanitzsch, Thomas. 2007. Deconstructing journalism culture: Toward a universal theory. *Communication Theory* 17(4): 367–385.

———. 2008. Comparing media systems reconsidered: Recent development and directions for future research. *Journal of Global Mass Communication* 1(3/4): 111–117.

Hanitzsch, Thomas, and Wolfgang Donsbach. 2012. Comparing journalism cultures. In *The handbook of comparative communication research*, edited by Frank Esser and Thomas Hanitzsch, 262–275. London: Routledge.

Harrison, Martin. 1985. *TV news: Whose bias? A casebook analysis of strikes, television and media structures.* Hermitage, Berks: Policy Journals.

Hawley, Amos. 1968. Human ecology. In *International encyclopedia of the social sciences*, edited by David L. Sills, 328–327. New York: Palgrave MacMillan.

Heclo, Hugh. 2008. *On thinking institutionally.* Boulder, CO: Paradigm.

Held, David. 2006. *Models of democracy.* 3rd ed. Cambridge, UK: Polity.

Herman, Edward S. 2003. The propaganda model: A retrospective. *Against All Reason.* www.chomsky.info/onchomsky/20031209.htm [last accessed: April 2012].

Herman, Edward S., and Noam Chomsky. 2002. *Manufacturing consent: The political economy of the mass media.* New York: Pantheon Books.

Hite, Katherine, and Paola Cesarini, eds. 2004. *Authoritarian legacies and democracy in Latin America and Southern Europe.* Notre Dame: University of Notre Dame Press.

Huang, Chengju. 2006. Transitional media *vs.* normative theories: Schramm, Altschull, and China. *Journal of Communication* 53(3): 444–459.

Hughes, Sallie. 2006. *Newsrooms in conflict: Journalism and the democratization of Mexico.* Pittsburgh: University of Pittsburgh Press.

———. 2008. The media in Mexico: From authoritarian institution to hybrid system. In *The media in Latin America*, edited by Jairo Lugo-Ocando, 131–149. Maidenhead: Open University Press/McGraw-Hill.

Huntington, Samuel P. 1991. *The third wave: Democratization in the late twentieth century.* Norman: University of Oklahoma Press.

———. 1997. After twenty years: The future of the third wave. *Journal of Democracy* 8(4): 3–12.

Hydén, Göran, Michael Leslie, and Folu Folarin Ogundimu. 2002. *Media and democracy in Africa.* New Brunswick, NJ: Transaction Publishers.

Jakubowicz, Karol, and Miklós Sükösd. 2008. Twelve concepts regarding media system evolution and democratization in post-communist societies. In *Finding the right place on the map: Central and Eastern European media change in a global perspective*, edited by Karol Jakubowicz and Miklós Sükösd, 9–41. Chicago: Chicago University Press.

Jamieson, Kathleen Hall. 1992. *Dirty politics: Deception, distraction, and democracy.* New York: Oxford University Press.

Jebril, Nael, Václav Stetka, and Matthew Loveless. 2013. *Media and democratisation: What is known about the role of mass media in transitions to democracy.* Oxford: Reuters Institute for the Study of Journalism/University of Oxford. http://reutersinstitute.politics.ox.ac.uk/sites/default/files/Media%20and%20 Democratisation_0.pdf [last accessed: March 2017].

Jenkins, Henry, David Thorburn, and Brad Seawell. 2003. *Democracy and new media*. Cambridge, MA: MIT Press.

Johnson-Cartee, Karen S., and Gary A. Copeland. 2004. *Strategic political communication: Rethinking social influence, persuasion and propaganda*. New York: Rowmand & Littlefield.

Juárez, Julio. 2009. *La televisión encantada: publicidad política en México [Enchanted television: Political advertising in Mexico]*. México: UNAM.

Kaid, Lynda Lee, and Christina Holtz-Bacha. 1995. *Political advertising in Western democracies: Parties and candidates on television*. Thousand Oaks: Sage.

Kalyango, Yusuf. 2011. *African media and democratization: Public opinion, ownership and rule of law*. New York: Peter Lang.

Kaplan, Richard L. 2006. The news about new institutionalism: Journalism's ethic of objectivity and its political origins. *Political Communication* 23(2): 173–185.

Kato, Junko. 1996. Institutions and rationality in politics: Three varieties of neo-institutionalists. *British Journal of Political Science* 26(4): 553–582.

Katz, Elihu, and Paul Lazarsfeld. 1955. *Personal influence: The part played by people in mass communication*. Glencoe, IL: Free Press.

Katznelson, Ira. 2003. Periodization and preferences: Teflections on purposive action in comparative historical science. In *Comparative historical analysis in the social sciences*, edited by James Mahoney and Dietrich Rueschemeyer, 270–301. Cambridge: Cambridge University Press.

Keane, John. 1991. *The media and democracy*. Cambridge, MA: Blackwell.

Kitschelt, Herbert. 2000. Citizens, politicians and party cartelization: Political representation and state failure in post-industrial democracies. *European Journal of Political Research* 37(2): 149–179.

Kitzberger, Phillip. 2012. The media politics of Latin America's leftist governments. *Journal of Politics in Latin America* 4(3): 123–139.

Klimkiewicz, Beata. 2010. *Media Freedom and pluralism: Media policy challenges in the enlarged Europe*. Budapest: Central European University Press.

Knight, Jack. 1992. *Institutions and social conflict: The political economy of institutions and decisions*. Cambridge: Cambridge University Press.

Krauze, Enrique. 1997. *La presidencia imperial: ascenso y caida del sistema político mexicano 1940–1996 [The imperial presidency: Rise and fall of the Mexican political system]*. México: Tusquets.

Kreps, David. 1990. Corporate culture and economic theory. In *Perspectives on positive political economy*, edited by James E. Alt and Kenneth A. Shepsle, 90–143. Cambridge: Cambridge University Press.

Krygier, Martin. 2015. God, bad, and 'irritant' laws in new democracies. *Media and politics in new democracies: Europe in a comparative perspective*, edited by Jan Zielonka, 119–136. Oxford: Oxford University Press.

Kurtz, Howard. 1998. *Spin cycle: Inside the Clinton propaganda machine*. New York: Free Press.

Lawson, Chappell H. 2002. *Building the fourth estate: Democratization and the rise of a free press in Mexico*. Berkeley: University of California Press.

Lawson, Chappell H., and Sallie Hughes. 2005a. The varriers to media openning in Latin America. *Political Communication* 22(1): 9–25.

Levitsky, Steven, and Lucan Way. 2002. The rise of competitive authoritarianism. *Journal of Democracy* 13(2): 51–65.

Lilleker, Darren G., and Ralph M. Negrine. 2002. Professionalization: Of what? Since when? By whom? *The International Journal of Press/Politics* 7(4): 98–103.

Linz, Juan J. 2000. *Totalitarian and authoritarian regimes*. Boulder, CO: Lynne Rienner Publishers.

Linz, Juan J., and Alfred C. Stepan. 1996a. Towards consolidated democracies. *Journal of Democracy* 7(2): 14–33.

———. 1996b. *Problems of democratic transition and consolidation: Southern Europe, South America, and post-communist Europe*. Baltimore: Johns Hopkins University Press.

Liotti, Jorge. 2014. The complex relationship between the media and the political system in Argentina: From co-option to polarization. In *Media systems and communication policies in Latin America*, edited by Manuel Alejandro Guerrero and Mireya Márquez-Ramírez, 100–121. Hampshire: Palgrave MacMillan.

Livingstone, Sonia. 2012. Challenges of comparative research: Cross-national and transnational approaches to the globalising media landscape. In *Handbook of comparative communication research*, edited by Frank Esser and Thomas Hanitzsch, 415–429. New York: Routledge.

Lloyd, John. 2004. *What the media are doing to our politics*. London: Robinson.

Loaeza, Soledad. 2008. *Entre lo posible y lo probable. La experiencia de la transición en México [Between the possible and the probable: The experience of transition in Mexico]*. México: Planeta.

Lowrey, Wilson. 2009. Institutional roadblocks: Assessing journalism's response to changing audiences. In *Journalism and citizenship: New agendas in communication*, edited by Zizi Papacharissi, 44–68. London: Routledge.

Lugo-Ocando, Jairo. 2008. *The media in Latin America*. Maidenhead: Open University Press/McGraw-Hill.

Lugo-Ocando, Jairo, and Juan Romero. 2000. From friends to foes: Venezuela's media goes from consensual space to confrontational actor. *Sincronía*. http://sincronia.cucsh.udg.mx/lugoromeroinv02.htm [last accessed: March 2017].

Lunt, Peter K., and Sonia M. Livingstone. 2011. *Media regulation: Governance and the interests of citizens and consumers*. London: Sage.

Mahoney, James. 2000. Path dependence in histotical sociology. *Theory and Society* 29(4): 507–548.

Mahoney, James, and Kathleen Thelen, eds. 2010. *Explaining institutional change: Ambiguity, agency, and power*. Cambridge: Cambridge University Press.

Mancini, Paolo. 1999. New frontiers of political professionalism. *Political Communication* 16(3): 231–245.

———. 2008. Comparing media systems. *Remarks presented at the Colloquium on Normative Theories of the Media*, Tempere, Finland, 26 July.

———. 2015. The News media between volatility and hybridization. In *Media and politics in new democracies: Europe in a comparative perspective*, edited by Jan Zielonka, 25–37. Oxford: Oxford University Press.

March, James G., and Johan P. Olsen. 1984. The new institutionalism: Organizational factors in political life. *The American Political Science Review* 78(3): 734–749.

———. 1989. *Rediscovering institutions: The organizational basis of politics.* New York: Free Press.

———. 1996. Institutional perspectives on political institutions. *Governance* 9(3): 247–264.

———. 2004. The logic of appropiateness. *ARENA: Centre for European Studies, University of Oslo.* [Working Paper (4)].Oslo: University of Oslo.

———. 2009. Elaborating the new institutionalism. In *Oxford handbook of political science*, edited by Robert Goodin, 159–175. Oxford: Oxford University Press.

Martin, L. John, and Anju Grover Chaudhary. 1983. *Comparative mass media systems.* New York: Logman.

Matos, Carolina. 2008. *Journalism and political democracy in Brazil.* Lanham, MD: Lexington Books.

———. 2012. Media democratization in Brazil: Achivements and future challenges. *Critical Sociology* 38(6): 863–876.

———. 2015. Public service broadcasting and media reform in Brazil comparative perspective. In *Media systems and communication policies in Latin America*, edited by Manuel Alejandro Guerrero and Mireya Márquez-Ramírez, 208–225. Hampshire: Palgrave MacMillan.

Mazzoleni, Gianpietro. 1987. Media logic and party logic in campaign coverage: The Italian general election of 1983. *European Journal of Communication* 2(1): 81–103.

Mazzoleni, Gianpietro, and Winfried Schulz. 1999. Mediatisation of politics: A challenge for democracy? *Political Communication* 16(3): 247–262.

McAnany, Emile G., Jorge Schnitman, and Noreene Janus. 1981. *Communication and social structure.* New York: Praeger.

McNair, Brian. 2005. PR must die: Spin, anti-spin and political public relations in UK, 1997–2004. *Journalism Studies* 5(3): 325–338.

McPherson, Ella. 2010. *Human rights reporting in Mexico*, PhD Diss., University of Cambridge, Cambridge.

———. 2012. Spot news versus reportage: Newspaper models, the distribution of newsroom credibility, and implications for democratic journalism in Mexico. *International Journal of Communication* 6: 2301–2317.

McQuail, Denis. 1983. *Mass communication theory: An introduction.* London: Sage.

———. 1992. *Media performance: Mass communication and the public interest.* London: Sage.

Merino, Mauricio. 2003. *La transición votada: crítica a la interpretación del cambio político en México [The voted transition: A critique to the interpretation of the political change in Mexico].* México: Fondo de Cultura Económica.

Merrill, John C. 2002. Classic books revisited: The Four theories of the press four and a half decades later: A retrospective. *Journalism Studies* 3(1): 133–134.

Merrill, John C., and Ralph Lynn Lowenstein. 1979. *Media, messages, and men: New perspectives in communication.* 2nd ed. New York: Longman.

Meyer, John W., and Brian Rowan. 1977. Institutionalized organization: Formal structure as myth and ceremony. *American Journal of Sociology* 83(2): 340–363.

Meyer, John W., and W. Richard Scott. 1992. *Organizational environments: Ritual and rationality.* 2nd ed. Berverly Hills: Sage.

Meyer, Lorenzo. 1995. *Liberalismo autoritario: las contradicciones del sistema político mexicano [Authoritarian liberalism: The contradictions of the Mexican political system]*. México: Océano.

Moe, Terry. 2005. Power and political institutions. *Perspectives on Politics* 3(2): 215–233.

Montoya-Londoño, Catalina. 2014. In search of a model for the Colombian media system today. In *Media systems and communication policies in Latin America*, edited by Manuel Alejandro Guerrero and Mireya Márquez-Ramírez, 66–81. Hampshire: Palgrave MacMillan.

Morris, Nancy, and Silvio R. Waisbord. 2001. *Media and globalization: Why the state matters*. Lanham, MD: Rowman & Littlefield Publishers.

Mughan, Anthony, and Richard Gunther. 2000. The media in democratic and non democratic regimes: A multilevel perspective. In *Democracy and the media: A comparative perspective*, edited by Richard Gunther and Anthony Mughan, 1–27. Cambridge: Cambridge University Press.

Mungiu-Pippidi, Alina. 2013. Freedom without impartiality: The vicious circle of media capture. In *Media transformations in the post-communist world*, edited by Peter Gross and Karol Jakubowicz, 33–47. Lanham: Lexington Books.

Murdock, Graham, and Peter Golding. 1999. Common markets: Corporate ambitions and communications trends in the UK and Europe. *Journal of Media Economics* 12(2): 117–132.

———. 2016. Political economy and media production: A reply to Dwyer. *Media, Culture & Society* 38(5): 763–769.

Nedeljkovich, Misha. 2008. Media coverage of elections news in the Republic of Serbia. In *The handbook of election news coverage around the world*, edited by Jesper Strömbäck and Lynda L. Kaid, 246–253. New York: Routledge.

Negrine, Ralph M. 2007. The professionalisation of political communication in Europe. In *The professionalisation of political communication*, edited by Stylianos Papathanassopoulos, Ralph Negrine, Paolo Mancini and Christina Holtz-Bacha, 27–45. Bristol: Intellect.

Negrine, Ralph M., and Stylianos Papathanassopoulos. 1996. The 'Americanization' of political communication: A critique. *The International Journal of Press/Politics* 1(2): 45–62.

Nerone, John C., ed. 1995. *Last rights: Revisiting four theories of the press*. Urbana: University of Illinois Press.

———. 2002. Classic books revisited: The Four theories of the press Four and a half decades later: A retrospective. *Journalism Studies* 3(1): 134–136.

———. 2004. Four theories of the press in hindsight: Reflections. In *New frontiers in international communication theory*, edited by Mehdi Semati, 21–32. Rowman and Littlefield: Lanham.

———. 2012. The historical roots of the normative model of journalism. *Journalism* 14(4): 446–458.

Ngara, Christopher O., and Edward N. Esebonu. 2012. The mass media and the struggle for democracy in Africa: The Nigerian experience. *Nordic Journal of African Studies* 21(4): 183–198.

Nieminen, Hannu. 2016. A radical democratic reform of media regulation in response to three levels of crisis. *Javnost—The Public* 3(1): 56–69.

Nordenstreng, Kaarle. 1997. Beyond the Four theories of the press. In *Media and politics in transition: Cultural identity in the age of globalization*, edited by Jan Servaes and Rico Lie, 97–109. Leuven: Acco.

———. 1999. Normative theories of the media: Lessons from Russia. In *Media, communications and the open society*, edited by Yassen N. Zassoursky and Elena Vartanova, 216–224. Moscow: IKAR.

North, Douglass. 1981. *Structure and change in economic history*. New York: W. W. Norton.

Oates, Sarah. 2008. Election coverage in the Russian Federation. In *The handbook of election news coverage around the world*, edited by Jesper Strömbäck and Lynda L. Kaid, 356–369. New York: Routledge.

O'Donnell, Guillermo. 1996. *Another institutionalization: Latin America and elsewhere*. Notre Dame: Kellogg Institute.

O'Donnell, Guillermo, Philippe C. Schmitter, and Laurence Whitehead. 1986. *Transitions from authoritarian rule: Latin America*. Baltimore: Johns Hopkins University Press.

Ogundimu, Folu F. 2002. Media and democracy in Africa. In *Media and democracy in Africa*, edited by Göran Hydén, Michael Leslie and Folu F. Ogundimu, 207–238. New Brunswick: Transaction Publishers.

Olsen, Johan P. 2007. Understanding institutions and logics of appropriateness: Introductory essay. *ARENA: Centre for European Studies, University of Oslo*. [Working Paper (13)], Oslo: University of Oslo.

Ostini, Jennifer, and Anthony Y. H. Fung. 2002. Beyond the Four theories of the press: A new model of national media systems. *Mass Communication & Society* 5(1): 41–56.

Papathanassopoulos, Stylianos, Ralph Negrine, Paolo Mancini, and Christina Holtz-Bacha. 2007. *The professionalisation of political communication*. Bristol: Intellect.

Park, Myung-Jin, and James Curran, eds. 2000. *De-Westernizing media studies*. London: Routledge.

Patterson, Thomas E. 1994. *Out of order*. New York: Vintage Books.

———. 2000. *Doing well and doing good*. Cambridge, MA: Joan Shorenstein Center on the Press, Politics and Public Policy, John F. Kennedy School of Government, Harvard Univesity. [Working Paper. *Faculty Research Series*].

Peters, B. Guy. 2005. *Institutional theory in political science: The new institutionalism*. New York: Continuum.

———. 2012. *Institutional theory in political science: The new institutionalism*. 3rd ed. New York: Continuum.

Peters, B. Guy, and Jon Pierre. 2007. *Institutionalism*. London: Sage.

Peterson, Theodore. 1956a. The social responsibility of the press. In *Four theories of the press*, edited by Fred S. Siebert, Theodore Peterson and Wilburn Schramm, 73–103. Urbana: University of Illinois Press.

———. 1956b. *Magazines in the Twentieth century*. Urbana: University of Illinois Press.

Pfetsch, Barbara. 2008. News management: Institutional appoaches and strategies in three Western democracies reconsidered. In *The politics of news: The news of politics*, edited by Doris A. Graber, Denis McQuail and Pippa Norris, 71–97. Washington, DC: CQ Press.

Pfetsch, Barbara, and Katrin Voltmer. 2012. Negotiating control: Political communication cultures in Bulgaria and Poland. *The International Journal of Press/Politics* 17(4): 388–406.

Picard, Robert G. 1985. *The press and the decline of democracy: The democratic socialist response in public policy*. London: Greenwood Press.

Pierre, Jon, B. Guy Peters, and Gerry Stoker. 2008. *Debating institutionalism*. Manchester: Manchester University Press.

Pierson, Paul. 2004. *Politics in time: History, institutions, and social analysis*. Princeton: Princeton University Press.

Pion-Berlin, David. 2005. Critical debates: Authoritarian legacies and their impact on Latin America. *Latin American Politics and Society* 47(2): 159–170.

Porto, Mauro P. 2012. *Media power and democratization in Brazil: TV Globo and the dilemmas of political accountability*. New York: Routledge.

Posner, Richard. 1993. The new institutional economics meets law and economics. *Journal of Law, Economics and Organization* (149): 73–87.

Powell, Walter W., and Paul DiMaggio. 1991. *The new institutionalism in organizational analysis*. Chicago: University of Chicago Press.

Preston, Paschal. 2009. *Making the news: Journalist and news culture in Europe*. London: Routledge.

Price, Monroe E., Beata Rozumilowice, and Stefaan G. Verhulst, eds. 2002. *Media reform: Democratizing the media, democratizing the State*. London: Routledge.

Puppis, Manuel. 2010. Media governance: A new concept for the analysis of media policy and regulation. *Communication, Culture and Critique* 3(2): 134–149.

Quintanilla, Víctor. 2015. Clashing powers in Bolivia: The tensions between Evo Morales's government and the private media. In *Media systems and communication policies in Latin America*, edited by Manuel Alejandro Guerrero and Mireya Márquez-Ramírez, 178–193. Hampshire: Palgrave MacMillan.

Randall, Vicky, ed. 1998. *Democratization and the media*. London: Frank Cass.

Rantanen, Terhi, and Nikola Belakova. 2015. Why is it important to study the media and politics in new democracies? In *Media and politics in new democracies: Europe in a comparative perspective*, edited by Jan Zielonka, 305–320. Oxford: Oxford University Press.

Raycheva, Lilia, and Daniela V. Dimitrova. 2008. Election news coverage in Bulgaria. In *The handbook of election news coverage around the world*, edited by Jesper Strömbäck and Lynda L. Kaid, 341–356. New York: Routledge.

Reich, Simon. 2000. The four faces of institutionalism: Public policy and pluralistic perpective. *Governance* 13(4): 501–522.

Reyna, José Luis. 2009. El sistema político: cambios y vicisitudes [The political system: Changes and challenges]. In *Una historia contemporánea de México*, edited by Lorenzo Meyer and Ilán Bizberg, 47–89. México: Océano, El Colegio de México.

Rhodes, R. A. W. 1995. The institutional approach. In *Theory and methods in political science*, edited by David Marsh and Gerry Stoker, 42–57. Basingstoke: Palgrave MacMillan.

———. 2009. Old institutionalisms: An overview. In *Oxford handbook of political science*, edited by Robert E. Goodin, 141–158. Oxford: Oxford University Press.

Rivapalacio, Raymundo. 1997. A culture of collusion: The ties that bind the press and the PRI. In *A culture of collusion: An inside look at the Mexican press*, edited by William A. Orme, 21–32. Miami: North South Center Press.

Rivers, William L., Susan Miller, and Oscar Gandy. 1975. Government and the media. In *Political communication: Issues and strategies for research*, edited by Steven H. Chaffee, 217–236. Beverly Hills, SAGE Series in Communication Research.

Rivers, William L., Theodore Peterson, and Jay Walbourne. 1971. *The mass media and modern society*. San Francisco: Rinehart Press.

Rivers, William L., and Wilbur Schramm. 1969. *Responsibilty in mass communication*. New York: Harper & Row Limited.

Rogers, Everett M. 1983. *Diffusion of information*. 3rd ed. New York: Free Press.

Rokkan, Stein, and Seymour Martin Lipset. 1967. *Party systems and voter alignments: Cross-national perspectives*. New York: Free Press.

Romano, Angela Rose, and Michael Bromley. 2005. *Journalism and democracy in Asia*. London: Routledge.

Ross, Karen. 2010. Danse macabre: Politicians, journalists and the complicated rumba of relationships. *The International Journal of Press/Politics* 15(3): 272–294.

Roudakova, Natalia. 2008. Media-political clientelism: Lessons from anthropology. *Media, Culture & Society* 30(1): 41–59.

Rubin, Bernard. 1958. *Public relations and the empire state*. New Brunswick, NJ: Rutgers University Press.

Sánchez Ruíz, Enrique E. 2005. Los medios de comunicación masiva en México 1968–2000. In *Una historia contemporánea de México: actores [A contemporary history of Mexico: Actors]*, edited by Ilán Bizberg and Lorenzo Meyer, 403–448. México: Océano, El Colegio de México.

Sanders, Karen, and María José Canel, eds. 2013a. *Government communication: Cases and challenges*. London: Bloomsbury.

———. 2013b. Government communication in 15 countries: Themes and challenges. In *Government communication: Cases and challenges*, edited by Karen Sanders and María José Canel, 279–312. London: Bloomsbury.

Sanders, Karen, María José Canel, and Christina Holtz-Bacha. 2011. Communicating governments: A three country comparison of how governments communicate with citizens. *The International Journal of Press/Politics* 16(4): 523–547.

Sartori, Giovanni. 1987. *The theory of democracy revisited*. Chatham, NJ: Chatham House Publishers.

Scammell, Margaret. 1995. *Designer politics: How elections are won*. Basingstoke: Palgrave MacMillan.

———. 1997. *The wisdom of the war room: U.S. campaigning and Americanization*. Cambridge, MA: Harvard [Working Paper].

———. 2014. *Consumer democracy: The marketing of politics*. Cambridge: Cambridge University Press.

Scammell, Margaret, and Holli A. Semetko. 2000a. *The Media, journalism and democracy: A reader*. Brookfield, VT: Ashgate.

————. 2000b. The media and democracy. In *The media, journalism and democracy: A reader*, edited by Margaret Scammell and Holli A. Semetko, xi–xix. Brookfield, VT: Ashgate.

Schiller, Herbert I. 1973. *The mind managers*. Boston: Beacon Press.

Schlesinger, Philip. 1990. Rethinking the sociology of journalism: Source strategis and the limits of media-centrism. In *Public communication: New imperatives; future directions for media research*, edited by Marjorie Ferguson, 61–83. London: Sage.

Schlesinger, Philip, and Howard Tumber. 1994. *Reporting crime: The media politics of criminal justice*. Oxford: Oxford University Press.

Schramm, Wilburn. 1956. The soviet communist theory. In *Four theories of the press*, edited by Fred S. Siebert, Theodore Peterson and Wilburn Schramm, 105–146. Urbana: University of Illinois Press.

Schudson, Michael. 2002. The news media as political institutions. *Annual Review of Political Science* 5: 249–269.

————. 2003. *The sociology of news*. New York: Norton.

Sending, Ole Jacob. 2002. Constitution, choice and change: Problems with the 'logic of appropriateness' and its use in constructivist theory. *European Journal of International Relations* 8(4): 443–470.

Servaes, Jan, and Rico Lie. 1997. *Media and politics in transition: Cultural identity in the age of globalization*. Leuven: Acco.

Shaw, Donald Lewis, and Maxwell E. McCombs. 1977. *The emergence of American political issues: The agenda setting function of the press*. St Paul, MN: West Publishing Company.

Siebert, Fred S. 1952. The Authoritarian theory. In *Four theories of the press*, edited by Fred S. Siebert, Theodore Peterson and Wilburn Schramm, 39–71. Urbana: University of Illinois Press.

————. 1956. The Libertarian theory. In *Four theories of the press*, edited by Fred S. Siebert, Theodore Peterson and Wilburn Schramm, 73–103. Urbana: University of Illinois Press.

Siebert, Fred S., Theodore Peterson, and Wilburn Schramm. 1956. *Four theories of the press*. Urbana: University of Illinois Press.

Sigal, Leon. 1973. *Reporters and officials: The organization and politics of newsmaking*. Lexington, MA: Heath and Company.

————. 1986. Who sources make the news. In *Reading the news: A Pantheon guide to popular culture*, edited by Robert K. Manoff and Michael Schudson, 9–37. New York: Pantheon Books.

Silva-Herzong Márquez, Jesús. 1999. *El antiguo regimen y la transición en México [The old regime and the transition in Mexico]*. México: Planeta, Joaquín Mórtiz.

Sparks, Colin. 2008. Media systems in transition: Poland, Russia, China. *Chinese Journal of Communication* 1(1): 7–24.

Sparks, Colin, and John Tulloch. 2000. *Tabloid tales: Global debates over media standards*. Lanham, MD: Rowman & Littlefield Publishers.

Sparrow, Bartholomew H. 1999. *Uncertain guardians: The news media as a political institution: Interpreting American politics*. Baltimore: Johns Hopkins University Press.

Steinmo, Sven. 1993. *Taxation and democracy: Swedish, British, and American approaches to financing the modern state*. New Haven: Yale University Press.

Stetka, Václav. 2012. From multinationals to business tycoons: Media ownership and journalistic autonomy on Central and Eastern Europe. *The International Journal of Press/Politics* 17(4): 433–456.

Street, John. 2001. *Mass media, politics and democracy*. New York: Palgrave MacMillan.

Stremlau, Nicole, and Ignio Gagliardone. 2015. Media, conflict and political transition in Africa. In *Media and politics in new democracies: Europe in a comparative perspective*, edited by Jan Zielonka, 289–304. Oxford: Oxford University Press.

Strömbäck, Jesper. 2009. Selective professionalisation of political campaigning: A test of the party-centred theory of professionalised campaigning in the context of the 2006 Swedish election. *Political Studies* 57(1): 95–116.

———. 2011. Mediatization and perceptions of the media's political influence. *Journalism Studies* 12(4): 423–439.

Swanson, David L. 1992. The political-media complex. *Communication Monographs* 59(4): 397–400.

———. 1997. The political-media complex at 50. *American Behavioral Scientist* 40(8): 1264–1282.

———. 2004. Transnational trends in political communication: Conventional views and realities. In *Comparing political communication: Theories, cases, and challenges*, edited by Frank Esser and Barbara Pfetsch, 45–63. Cambridge: Cambridge University Press.

Swanson, David L., and Paolo Mancini. 1996. *Politics, media, and modern democracy: An international study of innovations in electoral campaigning and their consequences*. Westport, CT: Praeger.

Swilder, Ann. 1986. Culture in action: Symbols and strategies. *American Sociological Review* 51(2): 273–286.

Thelen, Kathleen. 2004. *How institutions evolve: The political economy of skills in Germany, Britain, the United States, and Japan*. Cambridge: Cambridge University Press.

Thelen, Kathleen, and Sven Steinmo. 1992. Historical institutionalism in comparative analysis. In *Structuring politics: Historical institutionalism in comparative analysis*, edited by Sven Steinmo, Kathleen Thelen and Frank Longstreth, 1–32. Cambridge: Cambridge University Press.

Thoening, Jean-Claude. 2003. Institutional theories and public institutions: Traditions and appropriateness. In *Handbook of public administration*, edited by Guy Peters and Jon Pierre, 127–148. London: Sage.

Tomlinson, John. 1991. *Cultural imperialism: A critical introduction*. London: Continuum.

Trappel, Josef, and Werner A. Meier. 2011. *On media monitoring: The media and their contribution to democracy*. New York: Peter Lang.

Trejo Delarbre, Raúl. 2001. Mediocracia sin mediaciones. Prensa, televisión y elecciones [Mediocracy without mediation. Press, television and elections]. México: Cal y Arena.

———. 2004a. Democracia cercada: política y políticos en el mundo del espectáculo [Trapped democracy: Politics and politicians in the entertainment world]. In *Democracia y medios de comunicación [Democracy and the media]*, edited by L. Maira, Leonardo Curzio, Yolanda Meyemberg, Raúl Trejo Delarbre, M. E. Valdés Vega and José Woldenberg, 95–123. México: Instituto Electoral del Distrito Federal.

———. 2004b. *Poderes Salvajes. Mediocracia sin contrapesos [Savage powers: Mediocracy without balances]*. México: Cal y Arena.

Trejo Delarbre, Raúl, and Aimée Vega Montiel. 2011. *Diversidad y calidad para los medios de comunicación. Diagnósticos y propuestas: una agenda ciudadana [Divesity and quality for media: Diagnosis and proposals: A civic perspective]*, edited by AMEDI. México: AMEDI, Cámara de Diputados LXI Legislatura.

Tunstall, Jeremy. 1970. *The Westminster Lobby correspondents: A sociological study of national political journalism*. London: Routledge & Kegan Paul.

———. 1977. *The media are American: Anglo-American media in the world*. London: Constable.

Tworzecki, Hubert. 2012. Political communication and media effects in the context of new democracies of East-Central Europe. In *The Sage handbook of political communication*, edited by Holli A. Semetko and Margaret Scammell, 450–461. London: Sage.

Ugalde, Luis Carlos. 2012. *Por una democracia eficáz: radiografía de un sistema político estancado 1977–2012 [For an efficient democracy: The story of a politcal system at a standstill 1970–2012]*. México: Siglo XXI.

UNESCO. 2014. *World trends in freedom of expression and media development: Regional overview of Central and Eastern Europe*. Paris: UNESCO.

U.S. Commission on Freedom of the Press. 1947. *A free and responsible press: A general report on mass communication: Newspapers, radio, motion pictures, magazines and books*. Chicago IL: University of Chicago Press.

Vaca, Maira. 2015. *Do old habits die hard? Change and continuity in the political-media complex at the outset of the Mexican democracy*. PhD diss., London School of Economics.

Van Cuilenburg, Jan, and Denis McQuail. 2010. Media policy paradig shift: Towards a new communications policy paradigm. *European Journal of Communication* 18(2): 181–202.

Van Cuilenburg, Jan, and Paul Slaa. 1993. From media policy towards a national communications policy. *European Journal of Communication* 8(2): 149–176.

Vartanova, Elena. 2012. The Russian media model in the context of post-Soviet dynamics. In *Comparing media systems beyond the Western world*, edited by Daniel Hallin and Paolo Mancini, 72–96. Cambridge: Cambridge University Press.

Vidal Bonifaz, Francisco. 2008. *Los dueños del cuarto poder [The owners of the Fourth Estate]*. México: Planeta.

Voltmer, Katrin. 2006. *Mass media and the dynamic of political communication in the process of communication*. London: Routledge.

———. 2012. How far can media systems travel? Applying Hallin and Mancinin's comparative framework outside the Western World. In *Comparing media systems beyond the Western world*, edited by David C. Hallin and Paolo Mancini, 224–245. Cambridge: Cambridge University Press.

———. 2013a. *The media in transitional democracies*. Cambridge: Polity Press.

———. 2013b. *Building media systems in Western Balkans: Lost between models and realities*. Sarajevo: Analitika- Center for Social Research. [Working Paper].

———. 2015. Converging and diverging pathways of media transformation. In *Media and politics in new democracies: Europe in a comparative perspective*, edited by Jan Zielonka, 217–230. Oxford: Oxford University Press.

Voltmer, Katrin, and Lone Sorensen. 2016. Mediatised transitions: Democratization in an age of media abundance. *Media Conflict and Democratisation Project*. [Working Paper]. www.mecodem.eu/wp-content/uploads/2015/05/Voltmer-Sorensen-2016_ Mediatised-transitions.pdf [last accessed: March 2017].

Waisbord, Silvio R. 2000. Media in South America: Between the rock of the state and the hard place of the market. In *De-Westernizing media studies*, edited by Myung-Jin Park and James Curran, 50–62. London: Routledge.

———. 2007. Democratic journalism and 'statelessness'. *Political Communication* 24(2): 115–129.

———. 2010. Latin America. In *Public sentinel: News Media and governance reform*, edited by Pippa Norris. 305–328. Washington DC: World Bank.

———. 2012. Political communication in Latin America. In *The Sage handbook of political communication*, edited by Holli A. Semetko and Margaret Scammell, 437–449. London: Sage.

———. 2013. Media policies and the blind spots of media globalization: Insights from Latin America. *Media, Culture & Society* 35(1): 132–138.

Wallis, Darren. 2004. The media and democratic change in Mexico. *Parliamentary Affairs* 57: 118–130.

Wasserman, Herman, and Arnold de Beer. 2006. Conflict of interests? Debating the media's role in post-apartheid South Africa. In *Mass media and political communication in new democracies*, edited by Katrin Voltmer, 59–75. London: Routledge.

Weaver, David. 1998. *The global journalist: News around the world*. Cresskill, NJ: Hampton Press.

Weir, Margaret. 1992. Ideas and the politics of bounded innovation. In *Structuring politics: historical institutionalism in comparative analysis*, edited by Sven Steinmo, Kathleen Thelen and Frank Longstreth. 188–216. Cambridge: Cambridge University Press.

White, Robert. 2008. The role of the media in democratic governance. *African Communication Reserarch* 1(3): 269–328.

Williams, Raymond. 1962/1966. *Communications*. Baltimore: Penguin Books.

Woldenberg, Jose. 2004. Consolidación democrática y medios de comunicación [Consolidation of democracy and media]. In *Democracia y medios de comunicación [Democracy and mass media]*, 193–206. México: Instituto Electoral del Distrito Federal/Sinérgia.

Wynn, Jonathan. 2017. An arson spree in college town: Community enhancement through media convergence. *Media, Culture & Society* 39(3): 357–373.

Zaller, John R. 1998. Monica Lewinsky's contribution to political science. *PS: Political Science and Politics* 31(2): 182–189.

Zielonka, Jan, ed. 2015. *Media and politics in new democracies: Europe in a comparative perspective*. Oxford: Oxford University Press.

Index

For Product Safety Concerns and Information please contact our
EU representative GPSR@taylorandfrancis.com Taylor & Francis
Verlag GmbH, Kaufingerstraße 24, 80331 München, Germany